GW00646272

WEST YORKS WALKS
KIRKLEES

Martin Brewis

Published by Sigma Leisure – an imprint of
Sigma Press, 1 South Oak Lane, Wilmslow, Cheshire SK9 6AR, England.

British Library Cataloguing in Publication Data
A CIP record for this book is available from the British Library.

ISBN: 1-85058-721-3

Typesetting and Design by: Sigma Press, Wilmslow, Cheshire.

Cover photographs: from top – the hamlet of Linfit; The 'Beacon' at Dewsbury and District Golf Club; Castle Hill from Farnley Tyas

Maps: the author
Photographs: John Holmes

Printed by: MFP Design and Print

Preface

I just love walking – but it was out of necessity in my early years. Indeed, I had to walk four miles a day to and from my primary school in the Rossendale Valley, Lancashire. As much of it was uphill on the outward journey, I developed strong legs and a healthy pair of lungs. Now, in so called 'retirement', I walk – as no doubt many of you who use this book do – for the sheer enjoyment of walking, though some would contend that my equal penchant for walking after a golf ball is a walk spoilt.

Kirklees is one of the five 'counties' of West Yorkshire, the others being Bradford, Calderdale, Leeds and Wakefield. Kirklees is in the south-westerly corner with, at its north-west end, Huddersfield 'fairest of all the English industrial towns' (Engels), from which radiate out the valleys of the Rivers Holme, Colne, Spen and Upper Dearne. The Spen valley is the location for the textile towns of Batley, Cleckheaton, Heckmondwike and Liversedge (affectionately known as 'Cleckmondsedge'). To the south are the well-known villages of Denby Dale and Holmfirth (of 'Last of the Summer Wine' fame).

I have worked in Kirklees for many years, but only recently taken to walking in Kirklees. I frankly confess that I have been astounded, or 'gobsmacked' as Yorkshire folk say, by the beauty and variety of the countryside of this part of West Yorkshire. At one moment, on clear days you can enjoy breathtaking panoramic views in all directions from the many ridges which rise well above 1000 feet; at another you are walking down into secluded and picturesque valleys where it seems that few feet have trod. Yet again, you can pause to view fascinating points of interest, including cruck barns, 17th century farms, mills, weather vanes, unusual wall and stile constructions, or clapper bridges. The variety of the walks and points of interest will, I hope, captivate you.

Acknowledgements

This book of walks owes much to the time and effort of others. I am much indebted to: John Holmes, a member of my regular golf fourball and my amiable walking companion – calm and unruffled even when the going got tough – and also the photographer, ever ready to snap another 'point of interest'; my 'checkers', all 'retired' secondary head colleagues, including Allan Newton, Bob

Etherington and Clive Watkins, without whose acute observational skills and advice the directions and maps would be less than accurate; to my son who, in the early days before he gained his first employment, accompanied me and – with his constant humour – rebonded our father-son relationship; to my daughter, who promised me a trek in Nepal if I completed the work; and most of all, to my wife who has patiently tolerated this overweening passion for walking – even in my sleep, allegedly!

Martin Brewis

Questions . . . and answers?

In some of the walks, I have posed some questions. They are collected together here for ease of reference. Some answers I know, but others frankly I do not. If you wish to be interactive, I welcome suggestions being e-mailed to: wywalks@yahoo.co.uk

N1: Oakwell (A): What is the origin of the village name Drub?
N2: Oakwell (B): What is the reason for the raised embankment?
N3: Birstall: What was the original purpose of the viaduct?
N4: Liversedge: Why are diamond shapes cut in the stone pillars?
N5: Hartshead: For whom is the burial place?

W1: Marsden: What is the meaning of 'fide sed cui vide'?
W2: Slaithwaite: What is the origin of 'Crimble'?
W3: Honley: What is the meaning of the reference to Silk?
W4: Thongsbridge: Deanhouse - what was its origin?
W5: Netherthong: What is a Thong in this context?
W6: Holme: What does IWI stand for?

C1: Farnley Tyas (A): When were the Castle Hill embankments built?
C2: Farnley Tyas (B): What was the purpose of the circular dip surrounded by a thick stone wall in the woodland?
C3: Thunder Bridge: Why is it known as 'Hospital Wood'?
C4: Wooldale: Why is the path proud to the land and with a shallow drain?
C5: Holme Styes: What are the classical allusions of Hades and Elysium?
C6: Hepworth: For what incident was Hepworth famous (infamous)?

E1: Briestfield: By whom was the Temple built?
E2: Houses Hill: Long Tongue Scrog Lane - why so named?
E3: Kirkburton: What was the original use of this type of pillar?
E4: Emley: What does 'Nulli Claudaris Honesto' mean?
E5: Shepley: What else can 'Carr' mean?
E6: Quaker Settlement: How did 'Pump Row Cottages' come to be so named?
E7: Denby: Why are Susannah Spring and Dunkirk Inn so named?
E8: Bagden: What is the appropriate meaning of 'Pingle' here?
E9: Cawthorne: What is that style of bridge called?

Contents

Central Kirklees

East Kirklees

How to Use this Book

Areas covered

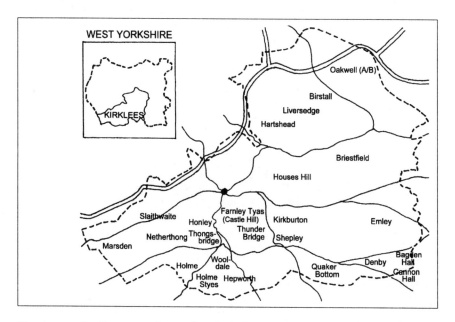

For ease of reference I have divided the 26 walks into four geographical areas:

North Kirklees (N): covers the valley of the River Spen, north of the A62 (Huddersfield to Leeds trunk-road), and bordered by Calderdale on the west, Bradford on the north and Leeds on the east. It is crossed by the M62 motorway – five walks.

West Kirklees (W): covers the valleys of the Rivers Colne and Holme, from the Pennines on the west to A616/6024 on the east – six walks.

Central Kirklees (C): covers the ridge that runs north and south and is bounded by A616/6024 on the west and A629 on the east – six walks.

East Kirklees (E): covers the Upper Dearne valleys, south of the River Calder, and bordered by A629 on the west, Wakefield on the east and South Yorkshire on the south – nine walks.

Distances

The walks vary in length from 4 to 11 kilometres (2½ to 7 miles) in length. All distances are inevitably approximate and a guide only. I have used metres and kilometres (with a conversion to miles in brackets) as the metric system is increasingly in use, and the walker covers kilometres more quickly than miles! At approximate points, the kilometres walked are indicated (in brackets) in the directions, and (in circles) on the maps.

Time

The time to complete a walk varies for all sorts of reasons. Every walker has her/his own comfortable pace; the terrain varies from level to undulating ground or to moderate / steep inclines and descents; weather conditions or seasons of the year change the state of the paths; you may wish to linger at points of interests. I have therefore assumed that the average walker will complete an uninterrupted walk at 3 kilometres (2 miles) per hour.

Maps and Descriptions

I have quoted from the Ordnance Survey (OS) Landranger (1:50 000), Outdoor Leisure and Explorer (1:25 000) Series with a grid reference for the starting point of the walk. The Pathfinder Series (1:25 000) is now discontinued and being replaced by the Outdoor Leisure and Explorer Series (but not all areas are complete at the time of publication).

The maps and the descriptions are intentionally very detailed in an attempt to keep you always on the right track. Indeed, each type of stile and gate is detailed so that you can recognise exactly where you are. I have used the shorthand (L) and (R) to avoid the constant repetition of the longer phrases 'on your left' and 'on your right'.

All the walks have been rewalked and checked independently of the author, but accuracy in every detail is impossible. I have been amazed at how much can change in a short time, e.g. stiles, gates and bridges change or simply disappear. The countryside also changes enormously with the seasons: paths which are clear at one season are overgrown at another; views obvious in autumn or spring are obscured by trees and hedges in the summer.

KEY to MAPS			
ᴄᴏᴏᴏᴏ Wall		Stiles : fence	ⵀ
ᴴᴴᴴᴴ Fence		stone/wall	ⵞ
～～～ Hedge		fence/wall	ⵟ
⟋ᴸ Metalled road/lane		metal	ⵞ
‒ ‒ ‒ ‒ Walker's track		metal bar	ⵁ
‒ ‒ ‒ ‒ Track,		pillar	ⵙ
～～～ Stream		ladder	ⵞ
～～～ Water		wall gap	⊔
⟩⟨ Bridge		Gates : fence	⊠
ⵖ⋏ⵖ Trees		metal	ⵘ
ⵞ Steps		farm type	⊠
▭ Cattle grid		kissing	∈
ᴴᴴᴴᴴ Railway		Gateposts	ⵏⵏ
	Drawings NOT to scale		

Terrain

I have indicated but not graded the sort of terrain over which you will be walking, and especially if there are steep stretches up or downhill. I have kept the amount of road walking to a minimum, assuming that walkers prefer countryside paths.

To the best of my knowledge all the paths are rights of way, but I have tended to keep off the designated 'Country Walks' or 'Ways', as they are documented in other publications.

The state of the terrain varies enormously according to the season and the current weather. You will find on all walks wet, muddy or boggy patches, and therefore, I would advise that you wear walking boots or tough waterproof shoes in all seasons. You may think shorts are suitable for summer walking, but beware nettles and brambles. Again, I would advise always taking a waterproof jacket and trousers, and other walking 'equipment' might well include a compass, whistle, extra pullover, food and liquid.

Parking and Refreshments

Most of the walks are accessible by bus, but I have not given details as routes, numbers and timetables can change unpredictably. The telephone numbers for Metro services are: (Huddersfield) 01484 545444; (Leeds) 0113 245 7676. There are also good train services from Manchester, Leeds and Bradford to Huddersfield, and along the famous Huddersfield to Penistone line (Tel. no: 0345 48 49 50).

I have indicated possible parking 'in the vicinity of'; if in doubt, please ask permission on the spot to avoid any offence or displeasure. Possible places to obtain refreshment have been listed on or nearby the walks, and there will be others that you can find; some only provide liquid refreshment.

Points of Interest

I believe that a walk is more than just walking. It is the 'points of interests' that really make the walk worthwhile and enjoyable. In order to make the text clear, I have differentiated it by putting the walk directions in normal type and the points of interest in *italics*. Please note, however, that this is a book of walks and there is no intention nor the space for it to be a historical or geographical guide. I have also put a summary description of the walk before the start of the directions.

The Countryside

Whilst the countryside is there for us all to enjoy, I would urge you to remember that for farmers and others the countryside is their business and livelihood, and so we all depend on mutual goodwill.

That said, walk on, and enjoy yourself in Kirklees – it contains many gems.

North Kirklees

Viaduct reflections, near Cleckheaton

N1: Oakwell (A)

Three Villages – Gomersal, Drub and Birkenshaw

Distance: 10km (6⅓ miles)

Time: 3 hours

Map: OS Landranger 104 (1:50 000), Explorer 288 (1:25 000)

Parking: anywhere in Oakwell Country Park off A652, grid reference: 213269

Terrain: meadow and field, woodland, farm track, path and short stretches of road – the walk is mainly on the flat with a moderate ascents and a descent back into the country park

Refreshments: at the café next to Oakwell Hall

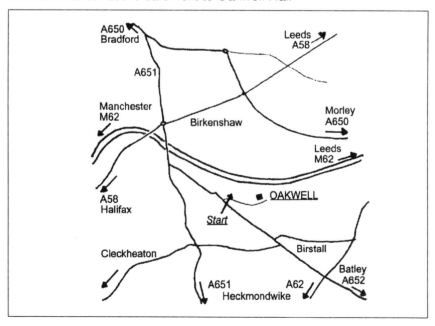

THIS walk starts and finishes in Oakwell Country Park, takes you briefly through the villages of Gomersal and Drub, and returns via Birkenshaw. The walk is generally easy with moderate ascents on the first half followed by high level views before you descend into and out of a valley to Birkenshaw. The walk back from there takes you under M62 back into the country park.

Start by returning to the car park entrance and onto the main road (A652). Turn left and, before you reach the boundary of Birstall, at a post box in the wall (L) cross the road and go straight up a path between fields. In places you walk over red brick and stone core. At the end, go along a wall (L) and up into Scott Lane. Turn right into the main road (A651) for 65 metres and left into West Lane. At the T-junction of roads, go straight on into Ferrand Lane with Gomersal Methodist Church (R). Go past the graveyard (R) and down between hedges (1km).

The path goes between red brick gateposts with a red post box (L) and then left past Throstle Nest Farm and up between fences/hedges onto a red shale track. At the top turn right along the main road *and past Bawson Cliffe House (R)*. In some 500 metres just before the double bend sign turn right on a public footpath over a fence stile in a hedge and down the field to a similar stile. Continue straight on down, going left of hawthorn bushes to veer left and under the bridge of a disused railway (2km).

In 50 metres go to fence stiles on either side of a wood bridge over a stream. Go up stepping stones and right round a wire fence to a zig-zag fence stile. *Turn round to your left and look over to see in the distance a house with a 'fox' weather vane.* Continue up the field alongside the fence (R) and over a fence stile and bear to the right-hand corner; bend left with the hedge to a fence stile in the top right corner of the field.

Bend left with the hedge (L), through a fence stile (L) and round a stone pillar, along a hedge (L) and up to the right and onto a track *with imposing stone gateways (R)*. Squeeze through the left-hand side of a wooden farm gate and turn left onto the road into Drub. *What is the origin of the name 'Drub'? There is a seat up to the right.* 70 metres on and round the left bend, take a path up right before and be-

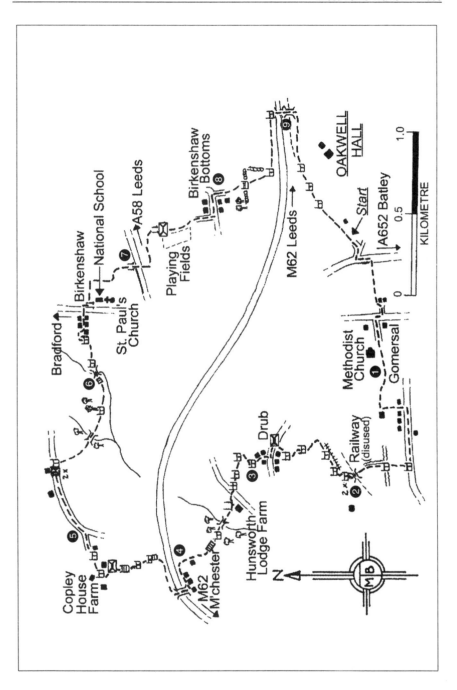

side the last stone house (R), taking the track round left *with a playground over the wall (L).*

At a right bend (3km) take the fence stile straight ahead and veer diagonally right over the field to a fence stile. Go left down the fence/hedge (R) to a fence stile and follow the hedge (L) to a zigzag stile. Cross the road (A58) turning right for 20 metres before going left up a red shale path alongside Hunsworth Lodge Farm (L). By the barns go slightly left, then right round the tree to take the left-hand squeeze stone stile. Go downhill to cross the stream at the bottom over a large stone slab and bear left to a fence stile. Go along a fence (R) and bear right up wooden steps. At the top go right round the edge of the field and take the path up at the corner of an adjoining hedge and fence with a gulley (R). Continue onto and along a broad track; at the top beside M62 bend left onto tarmac (4km).

In 100 metres turn right and cross the motorway and walk on for 500 metres. As the left bend ends cross the road and take the stone steps (L) up to a fence stile onto a public footpath. Walk alongside a hedge (R) and go over a fence stile *with a water trough (R)*, and on to a ladder fence stile. *Stop here to take in the view to north, west and south.* Go right round a hedge to a metal gate, then straight on to a fence stile between buildings. Turn right at Lower Park House Farm (L) onto the concrete Lower Lane between buildings. Go over a fence stile with a metal farm gate (L). *Copley House Farm (L) has an interesting blocked up window on its west gable.* Continue up Lower Lane until you join the main road (5km).

Continuing straight on you approach some houses on your left and opposite no. 495 (Hitchcock) there is a signpost to the right to Birkenshaw. Cross the road and go right over a fence stile beside double metal gates (R) onto a broad shale track. Go down and round to the left to go over a fence stile next to a metal gate (L). Go over a stream and veering right aim for the church spire peeping out of the top of the trees; take a slightly left curve across the field towards the biggest tree in the hedge ahead. Go over the stream and a fence stile. Keep across up the field moving in line with the telecommunications mast ahead. Aim to go through and under hawthorn bushes to steps up and over a slab stone bridge and fence stile (6km).

Carry on up a moderately steep slope with a wall (R). Halfway up, cross a fence stile. At the top follow the garden wall round left and then right, and go left into and along the road. At the main road turn right for 50 metres. Cross the road and go straight through two wooden posts into a ginnel. *Worth seeing down the road is the National School (L), built (AEDificatum) in AD 1838, with St Paul's Church further on.* Down the ginnel you pass a bowling green and playground (R). Turn right at the lamp-post and telegraph pole and go between walls and hedges past two sets of metal barriers. Bend left with the fence and along the road for 50 metres before turning right into Prospect Lane. After Greentrees (R) the road broadens out; at the bottom go into a ginnel right of a house and at the end squeeze past a large stone gatepost and wall (7km).

Cross A58 into Kingsley Drive. Take the first left into Kingsley Avenue. Bend right at the far end and turn immediately right through metal gates into a games field. Bear left along the hedge aiming for the far left corner. Go past posts into a ginnel between fences. At the junction with the road (Bottoms Lane) *on the opposite right corner is a period residence, Upper House.* Pass allotments (L) and turn left into Moor Lane and pass Croft Farm (R).

At Birkenshaw Bottoms Methodist Church (R) turn right (8km) down the road which becomes a tarmac footpath, then a grassy one between walls. At the bottom go over a wall stile *with a large stone block on its downside. It is at this point that you feel the full force of the sound of the M62!* Head diagonally left for the blue motorway sign to a fence stile and then go left between fences alongside M62 up to a fence stile. Turn right and go down and under M62, on between fences under the pylons and across the bridge over the disused railway into the Country Park (9km).

You can now take several ways back to your car: straight on past the Tree Garden (R), Oakwell Hall and veer right onto an 'access' path which zigzags through a hawthorn hedge and over a stream to the car park. Alternatively, turn right passing the Wildlife Garden (L) and follow the route of the railway, taking in three fence stiles on your way down to the car park at the end (L) (10km).

Oakwell Country Park

Oakwell Hall is an Elizabethan manor house with the date 1583 and initials IB over the doorway; it is furnished as the home of the Batt family in the 1690s. It is open Mon-Fri: 11am to 5 pm, and Sat-Sun: noon to 5 pm. Curator (01924 474926).

The Country Park has a number of interesting features: a museum, adventure playground, discovery trail and willow labyrinth, as well as a Wildlife Access Garden and a Tree Garden.

Adwalton Moor, not far away, was the site of a Civil War battle in 1643 between the Parliamentarians and Royalists.

Oakwell Hall

N2: Oakwell (B)

The 'Crosses' – East Bierley

Distance: 11km (7 miles)

Time: 3½ hours

Map: OS Landranger 104 (1:50 000), Explorer 288 (1:25 000)

Parking: anywhere in Oakwell Country Park off A652, grid reference: 213269

Terrain: meadow and field, woodland, farm track, path and short stretches of road – the walk is mainly on the flat with a couple of moderate ascents and a descent back into the country park

Refreshments: at the café next to Oakwell Hall and at The New Inn in East Brierley

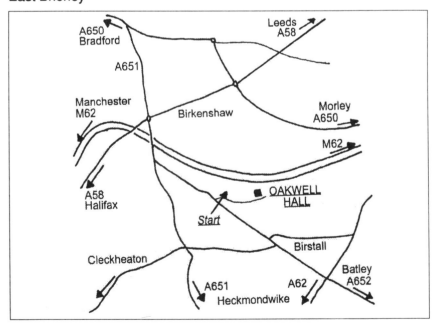

THIS walk is about the same length as Oakwell (A): it starts and finishes in Oakwell Country Park. It takes you up through the village of Birkenshaw, then down into a valley before taking you up and at a relatively high level onwards and through the attractive village of East Bierley and an area of 'cross' history. You return by a route over open country to the east of Birkenshaw before dropping down under M62 and back through the Country Park.

With your back to the car park entrance move left through bushes to turn right onto the line of the old dismantled railway. On your way up you cross three fence stiles and over a stream before passing the Wildlife Garden (R). At the T-junction (1km) turn left over the railway bridge and go up between fences and past a wooden farm gate and under M62. At the far side turn left over a fence stile and between fences follow the motorway. At the far end cross a fence stile, turn right and with your back to the motorway veer diagonally left up and over the field to a wall stile *with a large block stone on its upside*. Carry on up the grassy track between walls and then onto a tarmac road.

At the junction (2km) turn left into Moor Lane and pass Birkenshaw Bottoms Methodist Church (L) and further on Croft Farm. Turn right into Bottoms Lane and go up past allotments (R). At the period residence, Upper House (L), carry straight on into a ginnel between fences, and at the end past posts into playing fields. Passing the swings (R) keep alongside the hedge (R) and at its end bear right and go through metal gates to emerge into a road. Turn left and almost immediately left again into Kingsley Avenue. At the T-junction turn right up into Kingsley Drive until you reach the main road A58 (3km).

Cross the road and squeeze past a large stone gatepost (L) and wall (R) into a ginnel. This takes you up into a road (Prospect Lane) which narrows at Greentrees (L). At the top turn left for 40 metres and then veer right into a ginnel. After a metal barrier *you could take the path left through the graveyard to pass St Paul's Church and turn right into the main road past the National School, built (AEDificatum) in AD 1838*; alternatively, you could go on through another metal barrier to turn left at the top by a lamp-post and telegraph pole, and

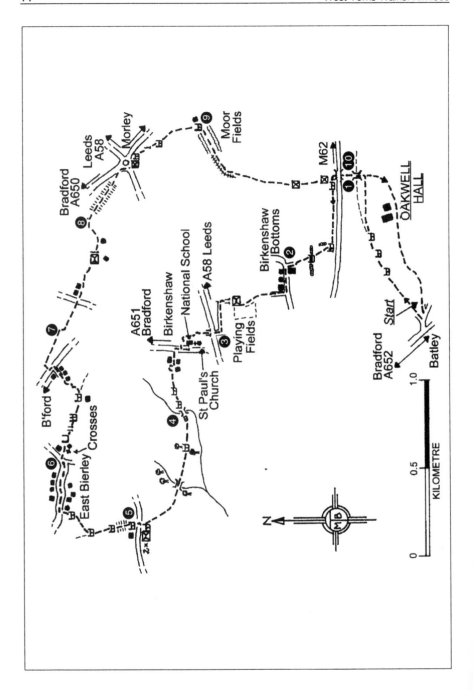

then go alongside a playground and bowling green (L). At the end pass through wooden posts (NB. *church and school down to left)* and turn right for 50 metres before crossing to go straight on down a side road. At the end follow the garden wall round to the right and then round left and downhill (4km).

Halfway down, go over a fence stile. Follow the wall (L) down and at the bottom go over a fence stile, slab stone bridge, down steps and go straight ahead up and under hawthorn bushes. When you emerge aim in a slightly right-hand curve for the tallest tree in mid-hedge ahead. Go over the fence stile and stream. Again head slightly right, curving upwards to a lone bush on the horizon between two pylons. Go over a broad track spanning a stream and a fence stile beside a metal gate (R). Bear up and round to the right on a broad shale path. At the top go over a fence stile to the right of double metal gates (5km).

Cross the road and slightly right onto a path signposted to East Bierley. The path is between hedges and after a fence stile between fences, going straight on a raised embankment to a fence stile – *what is the reason for this raised embankment?* Carry straight on to a fence stile and bend right with the wall (later a hedge) continuing on some way to a fence stile with a metal gate (R). Veer left onto a concrete lane between a hedge (L) and houses (R). You are now in the village of East Bierley. Turn right into Raikes Lane; where this becomes South View Road, The New Inn is across the road.

Continue past Manor Farm and Court (R) and further on the Cricket Club. At the Green ahead (6km) walk diagonally right over a stone slab pavement. *Note the double stocks (L).* Over the road go up the tarmac lane past the Methodist Free Church (L) to an area, Bierley Marsh, known for its 'crosses': *the centre piece is a fat stone stump (R), known as the 'cup and saucer', once topped by a cross; 'cross' pond (L) is now inhabited by ducks, with their individual 'houses', and buildings around the Green have names such as Cross Cottage and Cross House (early 17th century), which has a niche high on its wall with EBE1662 – all part of the Heritage Trail.*

At the far end of the pond go through a gap in the wall into a ginnel, then squeeze between stone pillars, on and over a driveway onto a path. Take the fence stile with three pillars, *one circular and*

Duck boxes at 'Crosses' Pond

note the well-worn step. Go over the field to a fence stile and turn left (*not* straight on) *past a house interestingly called 'The Other Side' (R)* along the farm track which winds left and right twice before turning right into Moorhouse Lane. At the main road (A651) turn left for 60 metres. Cross the road and go to the right of the bus shelter over the disused railway, and turn right. The path goes straight onto Tong Moor Local Nature Reserve alongside the cutting of the railway (R). Further on (R) *see the huge stone slabs – maybe of a platform.*

At the end (7km) take the track to the right over what used to be a bridge and round to the left. At a bend right, do *not* go straight on along a paved track beside the fence (L), but take the slightly right-hand track across open land, joining a main track from Tong Moorside by a hawthorn bush (L). At the road, go straight over onto the public bridleway of Hodgson Lane. By Springfield Farm (R) go through the gap beside a metal gate (R). Further on go round left and right bends past a farm (8km) and you come to a concrete lane – you may care to climb and walk along the embankment (L) to get a better view. At the end veer right onto the main road and on to the roundabout; go to the right and immediately cross A58 and up brick setts opposite and through a fence gate. Go up round left, then right of a wall to a fence stile. Go up and along the edge of an embankment; at a wooden gatepost veer down right of a hawthorn hedge and on to a fence stile beside a horse fence (R). Carry on past other similar fences.

Once on open ground at a solitary stone gatepost, pause *to take in the whole vista from Wakefield ahead to beyond Halifax away to your right; to your left is Adwalton Moor, the site of a Civil War battle in 1643.* Go straight ahead towards a bushy tree above a concrete barn with a corrugated roof (it comes into view as you cross the field), where there is a fence stile (9km). Turn right and go between hedges down the bridleway which becomes a path alongside a fence (R). Go with the left bend and come eventually to a fence gate beside open posts. Carry on downhill and go through a fence gate to go under the M62 (10km).

Go on between fences under the pylons and across the bridge over another disused railway into the Country Park. You can now take several ways back to your car: straight on past the Tree Garden (R), Oakwell Hall and veer right onto an 'access' path which zigzags through a hawthorn hedge and over a stream to the car park; or, turn right passing the Wildlife Garden (L) and follow the route of the railway, taking in three fence stiles on your way down to the car park (L) (11km).

Oakwell Country Park

See previous walk – Oakwell (A)

East Bierley

The 'cross' was erected by a Norman Lord of the Manor in memory of a peasant killed by his horse.

Raikes Lane was known for "going down to Ginnie's" – Ginnie being the lady of the tavern, very popular with men, but not with women!

N3: Birstall

The View from Popeley Fields – via Cleckheaton and Gomersal

Distance: 8.5km (5⅓ miles)

Time: at least 2½ hours

Map: OS Landranger 104 (1:50 000), Explorer 288 (1:25 000)

Parking: in the vicinity of St Peter's Church, Birstall, which is located in the western angle of A652 and A643, grid reference: 218263

Terrain: meadow and field, farm track, path and stretches of road – the walk is undulating over easy ground with a couple of short and moderate uphill stretches

Refreshments: close to the start of the walk: Black Bull Inn behind St Peter's Church, California Inn and The Bull's Head near Little Gomersal

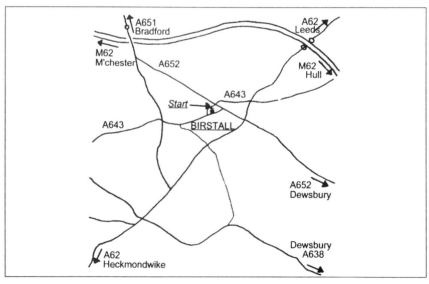

THIS walk is relatively easy, taking you through pleasant country-side whilst being close to habitation. Early on in the walk from Popeley Fields you get some splendid panoramic views mainly in a southerly direction. You also pass by some older parts, especially Halls, in former hamlets, and you end up at a small fisherman's pond opposite the church.

Starting with St Peter's Church to your left go up the road and round left in front of the Black Bull Inn *allegedly famed for its Luddite trial. The west end of the church is quite photogenic.* Carry on past Lych Gate Cottage (L) and at the road cross to go steeply up Garfitt Hill. Again, cross a road and go over wall stile to the left of ornate double gates ahead. Go up along a wall (L) and later a fence. At a lone wooden post turn right up the field and then left at the fence. *You are now high up crossing Popeley Fields from where you gain a fine panoramic view over Heckmondwike (L), to Emley Mast, Littletown and Liversedge, to Cleckheaton, Castle Hill and Holme Moss (ahead) and over to the right Gomersal and in the distance Ovenden Wind Farm beyond Halifax* (1km).

At crosstracks, go straight on over a fence stile beside a metal gate (R), and on down a path. At another set of crosstracks/stiles again go over a fence stile and straight on down between bushes. Shortly, in 40 metres, take the right fork through the hedge and go down between buildings to the California Inn (L) at the main road. Walk right for 200 metres, then left into Lower Lane, signposted to Little Gomersal. At the crossroads go over and past The Bull's Head (L). *You pass Gomersal Lodge (L) with its imposing entrance and post box with horseman and post-horn* (2km).

Taking the bend right past Little Gomersal House and Cottage (L) go left into a ginnel, beyond no.33 Lowfold. Go round left, then turn right and over a fence stile on the Brontë Way. As you go on along a raised embankment to a fence stile, *take in the view leftwards, including Castle Hill peeping through in the middle horizon.* Cross the field and go through a small fence gate to go straight over the crosspaths and along a hedge (R) past a fence stile. At the end of the hedge go past a pillar stile (L) and veer left over the field to a fence stile and down steps. Turn right and go between hawthorn bushes on a broad track.

Going between a fence (L) and wall (R) (3km), bend right and past
(1998) The Barn (L), through metal gates on a farm track. At the junction with the road, *opposite are the remains of old gateways with
postholes and a fence of old construction.* Turn left and go down into
and up out of the dip to join with Gomersal Lane. Turn up right for
100 metres before crossing the road and turning left down a road
(Freight Route) – *the splendid Spen Hall is just further up the main
road.* Then veer left down a tarmac path with wire fence (R). Don't go
left (onto a viaduct), but bear right down a path with a wooden fence
(L). At the bottom, bearing left to go under willows, you go past a
pond (L) *with a fine view of the viaduct* (4km) – *what was the original
purpose of this viaduct?*

Turn right onto a path which goes through a low wall and over old
wooden sleepers and on between fences to a zigzag fence stile with
metal tubes as its base. Keeping the stream on your left, go past two
standing stones. Veer left to cross the stream over a wooden bridge;
then wind round on a flagged pavement to turn right on a track back
over the stream. Go straight on up alongside an adjoining stream (L)
with a high wall (R). At the top turn left into Cliffe Lane and go
straight on and into a ginnel ahead. At the end of it, turn right up
alongside houses. 200 metres on go through the gap between a wall
(L) and bush (R), and on past a fence (R) to a fence stile. Further on at
the end of fences (L) take another fence stile (5km).

Go across the field for 150 metres, then turn right over a stone slab
bridge with white handrails across a stream and over a fence stile.
The stream cascades over slabs (R). Go up and in 30 metres take a
fence stile to the right. Carry on up and over the field keeping to the
hedge (L). In mid-field go left over a fence stile and follow the hedge
(R). Go over a fence stile with wood pillars. *Over to your right you will
see a 'fox' weather vane on a house roof.* Go left of hawthorn bushes
and then go round to the right and down over stone slabs and fence
stiles on either side of a wooden bridge over a stream. Shortly you go
under the bridge of a disused railway. Go uphill, veering slightly
right and keeping the hedge of bushes on the left. Cross a fence stile
in a hedge. Continue over the next field to cross a similar stile to the
road (6km).

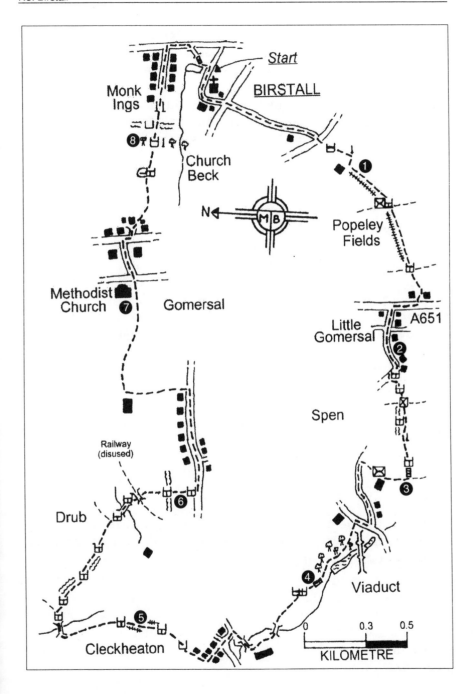

Turn left and walk up the road. In 250 metres just past the ornate gates of Bawson Cliffe (L) turn left onto a red shale track and go on down between hedges and fences until you reach Throstle Nest Farm at the bottom. Turn right through red brick gateposts and continue uphill on the farm track. Follow it round, eventually passing between walls with a graveyard (L). Gomersal Methodist Church (L), *known from its shape as the 'Pork Pie'* is at the top of Ferrand Lane (7km).

At the junction carry straight on and down West Lane. At the end are *houses of former times – Gomersal Hall (L) and Sigston House (opposite)*. Turn right (A651) for 65 metres and left into Scott Lane. Veer for the right hand footpath passing a house (opposite) *with the Latin motto 'semper fidelis pro libertate'*. Go right round the bottom of the graveyard (R) and squeeze between a wall (L) and hedge (R). Continuing along a hedge (R), go round left down between walls. At the bottom squeeze between the gap in the wall with an old metal kissing gate (L), and go over a fence stile and diagonally across a field. Step over a metal bar stile beside a lone standing stone (R) in a line of trees. Go past a lone stile in a wide gap in a hedge and eventually squeeze between pillars and go down a track between fences/hedges (8km).

Join a road (Monk Ings) until you reach the main road (A652). Turn right until opposite Cambridge Road (L) veer right down a path to cross a wooden bridge over a stream. Go up some steps and left round a pond, *which seems to be a favourite with fishermen*, and back to wherever you have parked your car (8.5km).

Whilst in this area you may care to pay a visit to Oakwell Country Park which is 700 metres up the A652 in a north westerly direction. Turn right into the car park.

N4: Liversedge

Twice over the Ridge

Distance: 5.3km (3¼ miles)

Time: 1½ hours

Map: OS Landranger 104 (1:50 000), Explorer 288 (1:25 000)

Parking: in a layby beside the cemetery on the road south of Hightown (A649) and north of Hartshead (B6119), grid reference: 189233

Terrain: meadow and field, farm track, path and short stretches of road – the walk is easy and undulating with moderate ascents and descents

Refreshments: not available on the walk, but at The Shears on A649 between Hightown and Littletown, and at The Star in Roberttown

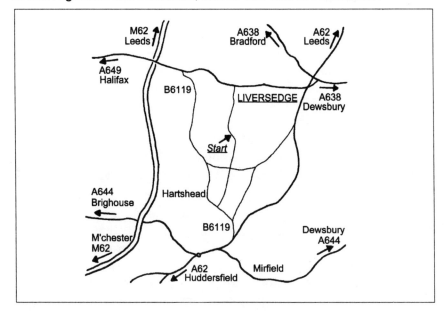

THIS walk takes you through gently rolling countryside into valleys on either side of a ridge between Hightown and Liversedge.

With the cemetery on your left, walk down below it and turn left onto a footpath past a pillar stone stile, with a metal gate (R). Go up alongside a hedge/wall (L). Take the right fork by a white post, keeping the hedge (R) and up under power lines. Towards the top of the hill at crosspaths turn right along the topside of a wall (R). Go through a slab stile, over a tarmac road *(Upper House Farm down right)* and down a track between hedges and over a stream in a dip. Continue up out of the dip.

At the top (1km) turn right onto Hare Park Lane *immediately past a house, no. 27, interestingly named 'Middle Deck'*. At the road junction, go straight over into Hightown Lane and past the First and Nursery School (L). At the end of the right-hand bend, take the steps (R) veering downhill into a small valley. Eventually you go down wooden steps (2km). Going between a fence (L) and hedge (R) cross a couple of sleepers. Continue straight onto a broad track and shortly go through a metal gate. The track is joined by a path coming in from the right, and then bends left.

Before the tarmac lane, turn right alongside metal fences (L) and walk past fence gates. Continue down along the Liversedge AFC field (L) with its floodlights. Go through fence gates and zigzag right and left under the railway. Go down right past a pillar stile (L). Continue along the fence (R) and walls (R) to an interesting stone stile *of three pillars with diamond shapes cut out of them. Why this shape?* Go immediately through a combination metal gate and fence gate. Follow the high brick wall (R), all the way round right, then left past another pillar stile and along a stone wall (R). Go to a fence stile and up and down wooden steps over an embankment (3km).

Turn right along the bank of a stream (L). *Ahead is a mixture of the old and the new: the old is an arched stone bridge with red brick parapets, the new is an overflow channel and tunnel (R). Across the stream here (L) is a blocked-up culvert.* At this bridge go through a fence gate and slightly right over the concrete track to a fence stile. Go through a field along a fence (L) and round to a sleeper beam over a stream. Cross a meadow to a fence stile in the left corner *opposite a red brick*

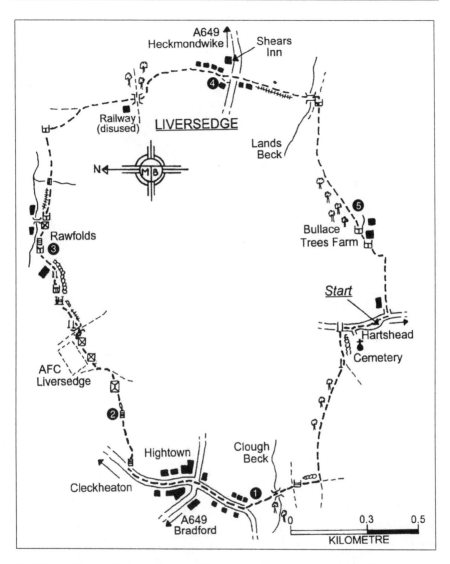

bridge with a reinforced metal lining. In front of it is the stone pier of a former bridge.

Turn right and eventually find your way up onto a broad track (Brontë Way) which takes you on past Primrose Farm (R) and a playing field (L) – *the tower of Littletown Church can be seen over the trees (L)*. Go under the bridge of a disused railway. Bear left and úp over

Liversedge: disused railway bridge

cobble setts and round right up the bridleway between fences and hedges. You eventually get up onto Primrose Lane; as it bends right carry straight on into a ginnel to the main road (A649). *On the left is The Shears Inn* (4km).

Go over the road into Balks. Carry straight on down past the houses and allotments (R) between hedges (L) and a fence (R). *Half-way down is a spring (L)*. At the bottom, squeeze to the left of a fence; take the stone bridge over a stream, and immediately turn right over a fence stile. The path from here is indistinct, but aim for the long line of hawthorn bushes and trees to the right-hand side of the farm ahead. Bear up left with them alongside a stream (R). At Bullace Trees Farm take a fence stile ahead and go up along a wall (L) past ivy-clad buildings (L) to a fence stile. Go up the path ducking under the bushes. Turn right onto a broad farm track. Go along this and passing Triangle Farm (R) turn right onto the road and to wherever you have parked your car (5.3km).

N5: Hartshead

Three-stone Stiles

Distance: 6.4km (4 miles)

Time: 2 hours

Map: OS Landranger 104 (1:50 000), Explorer 288 (1:25 000)

Parking: take B6119 (Far Common Lane) between A62 at Mirfield Moor and the village of Hartshead, on Fall Lane about 200 metres from Holly Bank School (L)

Terrain: meadow and field, farm track, path and short stretches of road – the walk is undulating with moderate uphill stretches

Refreshments: The Gray Ox at Peep Green, above Hartshead, The Star in Roberttown or The Three Nuns on A62 near Colne Bridge roundabout

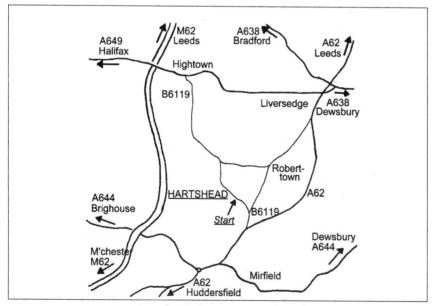

Hartshead church

THIS walk takes you through attractive countryside around the village of Hartshead, high up past the parish church at (High) Hartshead before taking you down a valley overlooking 'Cleckmondsedge' and returning you over the ridge at Roberttown. A special feature of this walk is the three-stone stiles.

Facing Hartshead on A6119 (Fall Lane) start by turning left down a lane between hedges and walls. Just before a cottage (L) *see the gatepost (L) with slot holes, splitting vertically.* Carry on past cottages (L and R) and go straight on through the metal gate, with stile (L) along the lane with telegraph poles (no access to cars on this 'private road'). Go through a large wooden gate onto a tarmac road and past Hartshead Hall Farm (L). As the road bends left, go straight on through a metal gate. 30 metres on, go right on a footpath down stone steps. *There is a fine view over the countryside to large farmhouses (L).*

Go into the dip (1km), through trees, over a stone bridge and up out of the dip keeping hedge (L). Just before fences ahead bear left over a stream and fence stile to go up the field with wire fence (R). Continue over a second fence stile and steeply up to a third. *The path to Three Nuns comes in from the left and there is a good view back to Castle Hill over parts of Huddersfield.* Go straight on towards Hartshead village on a former trackway, now grassy, between stone

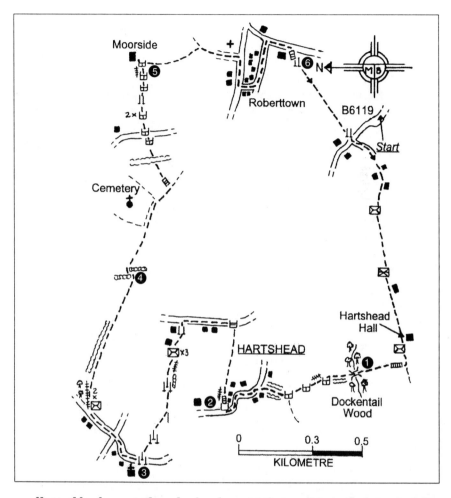

walls and hedges, and under bushes. At the road junction go straight on. *The garage of the house on the left, aptly named 'Pigatu', has a weather vane of a pig and two piglets.* Bend left and right with the road and, as it dips, turn right through a wall gap up steps onto a public footpath (2km).

Go along a fence (L) and at the top of the field go over an old fashioned well-worn stone stile, then turn left into the road. Over the crest of the road take the footpath left to Peep Green Farm. Go between metal posts taking the lane past garages (R) and through a series of metal gates. Then go past a series of old stone gateposts. Walk with the fence (L), cross a fence stile and go straight on keeping a holly hedge and wall (L). Go through a zigzag three-stone stile. At a telegraph pole halfway along, veer right across a field towards the church and another, but different, three-stone stile. Continue along a hedge (L) to yet another three-stone stile at the road (3km). *Pause here to view the horse mounting steps and stocks (L), and St Peter's Parish Church, Hartshead, across the road. In the churchyard is an old knarled tree stump.*

Turn right along the road past the church and bear right to the road junction. Go straight over the crossroads. In some 200 metres, squeeze right between a fence (L) and double metal gates, and pass on your left *a tiny burial ground in a copse – for whom?* Continue on along a broad path with hedge (L). *You gain extensive views over to Liversedge – or 'Cleckmondsedge', as the area including Cleckheaton and Heckmondwike is sometimes affectionately called.* Eventually you come to stone walls; zigzag between them (4km).

Go on up a long stony track, eventually between stone walls, *over the left one being the cemetery with imposing gates.* Some 30 metres beyond this, beside an elderberry bush, turn left down steps and go across a field; go over a stream through a hawthorn hedge and bear left to a fence stile in a similar hedge. Crossing the road go over a fence stile by a metal gate (L). Go across a field and fence stiles on either side of a ditch. Veer leftish and between concrete poles. Cross two fields and two fence stiles. Go alongside a wire fence (L) to a fence stile at Moorside Farm (5km).

Turn right up the lane and go past ruined buildings (R) and towards the top bear right onto a tarmac road. Carry on past Roberttown Parish Church of All Saints (L). Turn right on the main road for 100 metres; at a telegraph pole turn left into Commonside between houses. Follow this round left and past old gateposts and slabs (R). At Roberttown Lane with The Star opposite turn right. Just past Halewood Vintners (6km) turn right down stone steps to a metal squeeze stile. Veer diagonally left across the field keeping the telegraph poles (R). *You get a fine view across Huddersfield, in particular the Zeneca works, to Castle Hill.* Eventually you come to a squeeze pillar stile through the wall and onto the road, and to wherever you have parked your car (6.4km).

West Kirklees

Wolfstones (Walk W5)

W1: Marsden

Tunnel End and Back

Distance: 11.5km (approx. 7 miles).

Time: 4 hours

Map: OS Landranger 110 (1:50 000), Outdoor Leisure 21 (1:25 000)

Parking: by a church at Hill Top (Lingards Road) south off A62 west of Slaithwaite or north off the B6107(Chain Road)

Starting Point: grid reference: 072132

Terrain: field, farm track, lane, stretches of road, some sharp ascents

Refreshments: at several public houses: The Olive Branch (A62); Tunnel End Inn; Hare and Hounds, Netherley

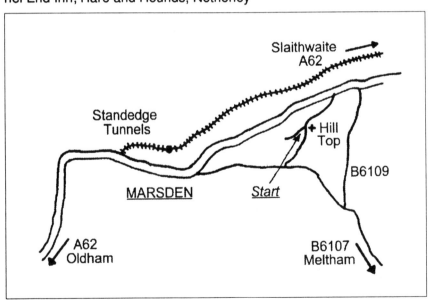

THIS longish walk, strenous on the return half, starts gently along stretches of the Huddersfield Narrow Canal, beside the River Colne and the main east-west railway over the Pennines. It affords you spectacular views of all three from various angles, and not least as the canal and railway disappear into the Standedge Tunnels at Tunnel End. The walk returns by steep ascents and descents above Marsden, before you come down from quite a high level on to an undulating path which allows you to take in extensive views of the Colne Valley.

At Hill Top start facing west with your back to a church and cottages on your left. After 50 metres down the lane take the fence stile (R) and down with intermittently a fence and wall on your left. Continuing down between walls, take care as it is rocky underfoot. Go over three fence stiles to stone steps which take you onto the main road (A62). Cross the road and turn right for 150 metres. On the left, go through a small fence gate and down over a fence stile (in the middle of nowhere!). Go left down a terrace between holly bushes above the river (R). *You may espy a heron, if you are lucky.* Go right over the fence stile onto a bridge over the river and then over the canal, to take the track up left to a junction of tracks. A flight of steps face you ahead, but you bear left down the track to go alongside the canal (L) until you pass on your right Waring Bottom Farm (1km).

At the junction with the road, turn left to go over the canal, then right to go through the gap onto the canal side. *Halfway up to the next lock, in some 100 metres, you can see on your left a small '6 mile' post – presumably the distance to Huddersfield. Lock 31e Booth has a fine tunnel bridge. Up on the left is a notice pointing you through Lingard's Wood to The Olive Branch, 300 yds left.* Just past a mill (L) take a flight of stone steps up left and go right over the bridge (2km).

Once over the bridge, turn left in front of the Sandhill cottages, over the stream and right up a track. Before you reach a white cottage, turn left and go along the embankment between the canal and Sparth Reservoir, up the stone steps and round right up the road. At the junction with the main road, go straight over a very overgrown stretch, and up steps and cobble setts onto the track under the railway bridge. *Just before going under, do look back to view the three fea-*

tures of the reservoir, canal and mill dam alongside each other. Bear left round and up past houses (R) and on to a lane (Moorvale) between walls. *Over the wall (L) you can see a most unusual narrow metal bridge / aqueduct taking a stream over the railway.* At the road junction go straight over and pass the backs of cottages *with flights of steps up to the doors.*

At the next bridge (3km) turn right keeping the telephone box (L), and go up the steps ahead onto a tarmac path with railings (L). Zig right and left up steps and through the gap in the wall. At the top turn left into the lane and past Dirker Bank Cottage (L). *There is an extensive view of Marsden over to your left.* After going past the backs of cottages (L) at Dirker you come to a house standing up on your right called Inglenook, *with an interesting Latin motto: fide sed cui vide – but what is its meaning?* Bear left steeply down Spring Head Lane; at the bottom turn right into Osborne Terrace and straight on along Reddisher Road past Far Rough Lee (R) following the road round. At Tunnel End Inn (R) turn acutely left to a picnic area laid out in front of the Standedge Tunnels (4.5km). You may care to rest awhile here.

When ready to resume your walk, at the left-hand end of the car park, take the curving path up left to a gap in the wall, up steps between fences and over a wall stile (R). Go left up the lane, left round the bend *(with a water trough on the right)* until you reach the main road (A62). Turn left: as you walk along *look to your left at the view of the railway tracks, canal, reservoir and overflow.* Continue for some 300 metres, crossing the road. Then halfway round a left-hand bend, immediately after a row of houses (R), by a telegraph pole turn right up stone steps between walls and on to two fence stiles on either side of a track. Go on up via occasional steps along a wall (L) until halfway up go left over a fence stile towards Old Mount Road.

Continue straight on beyond the line of the wall (L) until you come to a fence stile at the junction of walls. Go left over the stile and a stream, then up along the wall (L) to a small metal gate. Keep right of the farm building: *having passed it, glance back to view its mullion type windows and porchway.* Continue up a grass track, somewhat overgrown even with rushes, between walls. *Take in the view of the mill down left and Butterley Reservoir ahead.* You pass old wooden

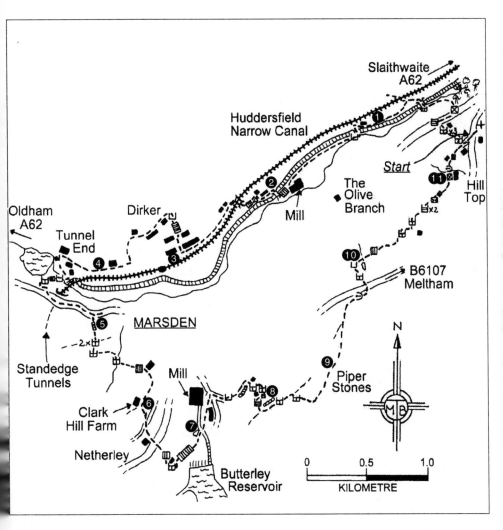

railway wagons (R) and a seemingly derelict 17th century farm-house *with IMH 1674 over its doorway* (6km).

Walk straight on along a terrace down to the road. Turn right and in 50 metres take a track diagonally left and follow it round with the metal railing, down between houses to join the road and the junction with the Hare and Hounds (R). Straight across and just past garages (R) take a small metal gate (R) and go all the way round left and down to a fence gate. Then take a very long flight of steps down below the dam wall. At the bottom go right across the bridge and left along a track. *Over the wall (L) you can see tanks, sluices, even another aqueduct* (7km).

Follow the track on through the mill premises. At the main road go straight over and up Ottiwells Terrace. At the end squeeze through the wall gap (L), up and along a wall (R). At the lane turn right uphill and straight on through a fence gate and left before Crowther Laithe Farm. Take the fence stile in the right corner, then steps up and round between walls to a wall stile. Up beyond this you turn left (8km) onto an undulating path following the wall (L), over a stream and a fence stile. Eventually bear down towards a farm and over a fence stile.

Carry on a farm track and before a metal farm gate take a fence stile (R) up the moor until it joins a broad track. Go left on this track past Piper Stones, an outcrop of rocks (R) (9km) and until you go through a wooden kissing gate and then round left onto Meltham Road (B6107). Turn right for 100 metres, then left down between walls and over a fence stile *(a pond away to your right). Go through a wide gap in the wall and veer right. Take in the view of the Sparth Canal basin (L).* Go through a metal gate and over a stream. From here (10km) the way zigs about and is often indeterminate: follow a wall (L) over tumbledown bits; take a fence stile and go right up a track between walls to a fence stile, and left down between walls; in 50 metres veer right over a wall, and again over tumbledown bits *(note the large stone blocks in the walls hereabouts).* After going over a wall and on stepping stones veer left down to a wall with a line of trees (L); here are two wall stiles and a gate beside a wrought iron farm gate. Steps take you down to a junction of ancient trackways.

After observing a stone trough (R), go straight on along Hollins Lane between walls past other wrought iron gates to a magnificent old deserted house *(note the low portals, the date 1758 and initials HWM carved in stone).* Proceed through a fence gate to a metal kissing gate and stones over a stream and another metal gate (11km). Large stepping stones take you along a wall (R) through a fence gate and past a farm *(inscribed IBSB 1757).* The track then takes you back to wherever you parked your car (11.5km).

Standedge Tunnels

The Standedge Canal Tunnel, opened in 1811, is one of the most spectacular feats of engineering in Britain. Before its opening, cargo had to be conveyed by packhorse over the Pennines. The tunnel on the canal from Hull to Liverpool was conceived by Sir John Ramsden, and was hewn with pickaxes, shovels and gunpowder. It is the longest tunnel in Britain, being 3 miles and 135 yards (4959 metres) in length, 17 feet high, 8 feet wide and 8 feet deep. On the eastern side, it has 42 locks making an ascent of 436 feet.

Standedge Tunnel

```
W2: Slaithwaite
```

Hill and Valley Views

Distance: 10.5km (6½ miles)

Time: 3 hours

Map: OS Landranger 110 (1:50 000), Outdoor Leisure 21 (1:25 000)

Parking: in a free car park on the north side of the canal basin, below the Parish Church, off Market Place, grid reference: 078139

Terrain: meadow and field, open moorland, woodland, farm track, path and short stretches of road – the walk is undulating with some moderate to steep ascents and descents

Refreshments: at the Shoulder of Mutton, Market Place, the Silent Woman in Nabbs Lane, and The Commercial in Carr Lane

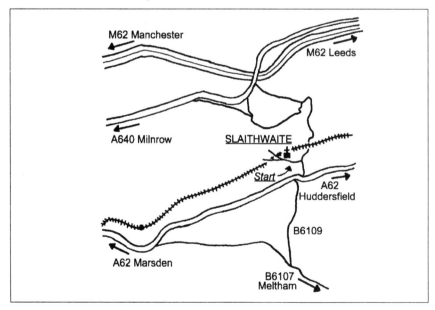

THIS walk takes you from the level of the canal up high above Slaithwaite. The second half takes you along part of the Colne Valley Circular Walk and alongside Moorside Edge, giving you extensive views over the Colne Valley. It brings you back down a delightful tributary valley past some of the older parts of Slaithwaite. There are lots of interesting features to view.

Starting from the car park with your back to the canal go up the steps to the right onto the road opposite the Parish Church of St James. Turn left and then veer left into Nabbs Lane and past the (unusually named) Silent Woman: *the building has an inscription SF1782, was formerly the Globe Inn, and in 1928 became the property of Bentley and Shaw's Lockwood Brewery.* As you walk on, *you will see house no. 11 (R) has weavers' windows at second storey, as do nos. 17 and 19 at first storey.* You pass into Holme Lane before the railway bridge and go steeply uphill. Turn right on a footpath over the dam head and the iron bridge over the reservoir overflow. *There is a fine old slim mill building down to your right.* Turn left between metal railings on to a track alongside the reservoir (L) and a run-off channel (R) at the bottom of gardens.

(1km) At crosspaths alongside a wall (L) carry straight on, winding your way round and up through trees. Turn left along a small reservoir (R) and round the corner *view a waterfall (L).* Go over a concrete bridge and veer left across a stream to go up and over a stony path. Turn right going between small walls. Go over a fence stile onto the road. Turn right over the bridge and then left on a signposted footpath squeezing between a metal gate and a wall. Carry straight on beside the stream (L) and wall (R). Do *not* take the bridge left, but continue further to squeeze between pillars (wood on left and stone right). The ground ahead may be boggy but there are some stepping stones (2km).

At a point where there is a little weir (L), the original way ahead is overgrown, so take a right-hand path. Go over a tumble-down wall. Beyond the power lines, *note a stone tunnel entrance up right, which was an overflow from an old reservoir above, now almost dried up.* Carry on until you come to a wall and have to go up right alongside the wall (L), *which halfway up has a gateway in it.* Go up past the

The former C of E Upper Slaithwaite School

house (L) and up stone steps between walls. Take either the lane, or the grassy path to the right beside hawthorn bushes, onto a road firstly of cobble setts, then tarmac (Tyas Lane). Cross a stream, which is culverted on the left. Going on steeply uphill you come to a signposted path (R). Ignore this to view the large house ahead (L). *This has been converted from Upper Slaithwaite Church School, which has the date 1845 inscribed over the right-hand door and VR over the left, a cross on the right-hand gable top and a weather vane to the left. The dedication states that the school was 'united to the national society for promoting the education of the poor in the principles of the united church of England and Ireland' (3km).*

Just beyond this 'school' turn right through a wide gap in the wall and go down to a small wooden kissing gate. Turn left and on to a wall stile with a fence stile on its far side. Veer slightly right across the field towards Emley Mast (on the skyline) to a stone pillar stile, and then along a wall (R) to a wall stile. Go across the field towards the farm going through a metal farm gate and up between fences to go through another such gate. Go diagonally over a short stretch of ground to a small fence gate. Going in front of the cottages you pass through a small turnstile.

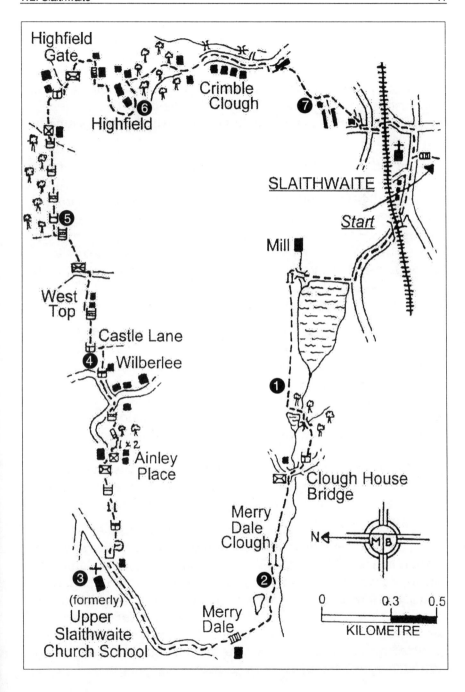

Turn right and then left through the buildings to squeeze through stone pillars beside a metal gate (L). Go down the field and through stone pillars. Go straight on down the stone steps – beware: they are well worn and slippery. At the bottom cross the stream on a stone slab bridge, then veer right up over slabs and left to a stone stile. Over it turn right onto the lane (Intake Road) and go to the junction of roads at Wilberlee (4km).

Veer left up into Tiding Field Lane and uphill *past a stone trough (L)*. As the road bends left, go off right over a wall + fence stile. Go along a wall (R) to another fence + wall stile. Cross the field to a post on the opposite side and down into a track called Castle Lane. Turn left up between the walls. At the top turn right over a fence stile. Cross a track and go along a wall (R) to a ladder type stile in the corner with wall stile. Pass left of the barn *dated AD 1872* and onto a dirt track past a cottage (R). At the end turn left up a lane for 35 metres, then right through a wooden farm gate.

Veer up left to the bottom of a wood (5km). Go left over a wooden ladder stile, uphill for a few metres, then turn right and head onto a grass track slightly left uphill to a fence stile. Go along a wall (L) to a wall stile beside a gorse bush. Continue on to a wall stile and then with the wall (R) and wood (L) to another wall stile. Go across a farm track to a small fence gate. Continue across the field to a fence stile, and go down right and up left round the building. Before the house with the balcony (L), at Highfield Gate, turn right and down through a metal farm gate and on between tumble-down walls. At the bottom go right through an iron gate; almost immediately the path turns left down between breeze block walls and goes on down the lane between trees.

At the next bend turn right and follow the road all the way round until it bends left to an open space in front of Highfield Cottage and Varley's Barn. Acutely on your right is the entrance to a path which takes you downhill into a wooded valley, past a red brick tank (R) (6km). *This is a delightful little valley/glen which takes you through and under fallen trees. From time to time you cross carefully constructed run-off water channels.* As you emerge from the trees into Rock Lane you pass (L) Swan Farm, *with its high retaining wall; if you glance backwards you will see that it has the original date of 1864, with a 1969 extension, and it is topped by a weather vane of a man with shooting dog and gun. Down below on your right is a house named 'Holywell'.* Just past a narrow bridge (L) over the stream, *look over the wall to see the little gorge with its cascading waterfall and shale banks.* Further on down on your right, *note the stone trough just before Ye Olde Crimble Cottage, with its bulging walls – what is the origin of 'Crimble'?* Down on the left, *note the stone steps down over a single slab bridge and up to the main road.*

Carry on past the bridge (L) on Rock Lane. Ignore the footpath (R). In 40 metres, as the lane widens with a row of cottages (R), turn right of them towards a double wooden garage. Turn left in front of it and walk on a grassy track along the backs of houses (L). Veer right between fences, taking the path uphill over slabs and steps (7km). You emerge on the topside of allotments (L) onto a road in front of bungalows (R). Having taken the right-hand bend, veer off left between wood and concrete (R) and red-brick sheds (L). Continue straight on down a path between walls. At the bottom, *glance back right to view a stone house with the inscription AEEB 1685.* Walk onto Olney Street and at the junction with Meal Hill Lane turn left.

At the crossroads glance left to see a row of old cottages. Go straight over into Bank Top; walk down over cobbles *past No.22 'Our Pad'.* Zigzag left and right twice down stone steps and under the railway bridge. At the junction veer right on down the road to the crossroads and turn right to wherever you have parked your car (8km).

W3: Honley

Woodlands and Ridges

Distance: 8km (5 miles)

Time: 3 hours

Map: OS Landranger 110 (1:50 000), Explorer 288 (1:25 000)

Parking: in a small layby at White Gate, immediately on the left after Mag Bridge on the back road from St Mary's Church, Honley, to Armitage Bridge, grid reference: 136124. NB. only room for two cars

Terrain: meadow and field, woodland, open moorland, path and stretches of road – the walk is undulating with some steepish ascents and descents

Refreshments: in the village of Honley

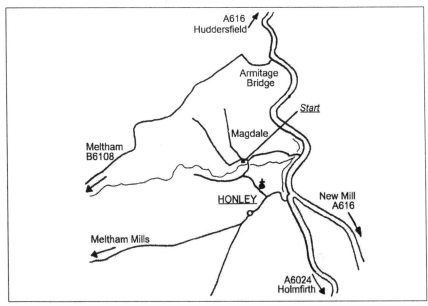

THIS walk, which describes a full circle round Honley Wood Bottom, is strenuous in parts with three steepish ascents. However, the rewards come, especially on the second half of the walk, in the views which are enjoyed in all directions from the ridge walk high above Magdale. Parts of the walk may be muddy.

Start by going in a westerly direction through the fence kissing gate on the left of a wooden gate. Go up the path for some 50 metres before squeezing left through the wall gap. Walk along the bottom side of the wood. As you cross a stream, *look up right to see water trickling down the rock face over lichen and moss.* After about half a kilometre through the woods a former mill building can be seen away down to your left across the stream. Take the left fork near the boundary of the wood, turning left down over stone steps towards the mill. The path goes between a fence (L) and wall (R) to a wooden bridge over Hall Dike. Veer right round the mill to go between the mill race (L) and the river (R) (1km).

Going on between fences you pass a horse dressage ring (R). At the end of the track opposite a gateway to another mill, turn left up Lea Lane, and going steeply up bear left round the topside of Magdale House (L). Go straight on up past a direction sign to Moll Springs (L). At the junction turn acutely right (into Woodbottom Road). As you walk along note: *the stout wall (L) containing some substantial stone blocks of varying size; and, in Woodbottom Cottage (R), the lower windows go down below ground level.* (If you want to get off the road, opposite semi-detached houses (R), you can go through a wall gap (L) and walk right winding your way through the trees, including holly; before you reach a wall you will have to find your own way back onto the road). Otherwise, continue to walk along the road. *At Granby Farm (R), the valley has widened out to give a good view across it.*

(2km) As Crosland Factory Lane goes down to the right, carry straight on up the lane ahead between walls. Ignore the gateway (R). Again, as the lane goes down (R) over cobble setts, go straight ahead onto a path and go left of a stone pillar. Take the path uphill into the bottom side of the wood – some of the paths, especially in the gully (R) may be rather muddy, but it is advisable not to stray too far away

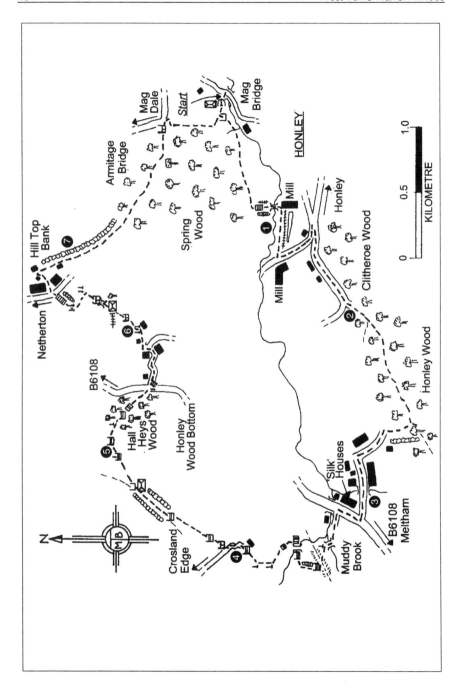

from it. Eventually the path ducks downhill (R) under an archway of holly bushes, though at one point you may have to track up left to get round the holly. Carry on generally keeping to the right-hand paths until you come to a stone wall with a house and outbuildings over it; turn right down the path alongside the wall (L), until you cross a stream and go left onto a road. Go past the Recycling Centre (R) and Sewage (Water Treatment) Works (3km).

Bend left with the road and pass Shaw's Export Services Centre (L). At the main road (B6108) turn right and walk past (R) houses in a row, named, *Shantung, Mulberry and Silk Mill House – why are these signs of former days?* Go to the bridge ahead: *on the parapet is a triangular milestone indicating Meltham Township B on one side and on the other South Crosland Township B.* Now turn back and at the sign (L) 'Bolling: The Coffee Roasters', turn right, cross the road and go down a track past a cottage (R). Veer right taking a stone bridge over a stream (Muddy Brook) and go up through a gate with a high stone pillar (R). Continue up and under the bridge of a dismantled railway.

Old boundary post for Meltham

After going between two wooden gateposts, turn right over a wall stile and follow the wall (R) round to the right. Go over the stream via a stone slab bridge and through a metal gate. *Note to your right how the stream has cut its way through rocky slabs.* Turn left up the fence and round a holly bush to steps over a wall. Go straight on up the field to a wooden sign on a stone pillar directing you up to the right. Going steeply up left of a hawthorn bush, and at another direction sign veer right towards a small fence gate, bearing left round the hedge to a wall stile in the corner (4km).

Go up the lane and round to the left; as it bends left again by a stone pillar (R) go right up to a fence stile by the side of the wall. Next continue up past a disused quarry (R) to a wall stile beside a worn barred gate. *Turn round here and pause to take in the view across the whole area of Meltham and beyond.* Go diagonally across the fields towards a stone slab stile in the wall corner ahead; keep the power lines (R) and the farm buildings (L). Go over and onto a track between walls. When you come to a metal gate (R), squeeze through the wall (R) to go diagonally towards the power pylon in the direction of Castle Hill on the horizon. Go through the wall by double poles. Finally, go over a wall stile with a wooden bar on the far side (5km).

Head in the same direction for a signpost and then straight down and over tumbledown steps into a wooded glen of mixed deciduous trees and holly. Towards the end of the wood go over a wall stile and down steps. *Left over the fence is a man-made pond.* Once out of the wood go between fences to a wall stile at the main road (B6108). Cross the road and turn right for 40 metres, then turn acutely left between walls and down steps to go right down Crosland Factory Lane. Just beyond the parapets of the dismantled railway bridge, *the stream (L) emerges into a little dam/weir.* At the T-junction turn left up lane and veer right eventually past a cottage (L) *with two chimney pots on its verge, and further on a lamp-standard outside no.26. Opposite (R) is a large stone trough set into the wall.*

At this point (6km) veer sharp left to squeeze between wooden posts. Then turn sharp right and go across the fields in the direction of weavers' cottages high up on the opposite hillside. In mid-field go over a fence stile, then right of a hawthorn hedge. Again, in mid-field squeeze between a metal gate and the left-hand wire (!) fence. Carry straight on left of an oak tree to a wood beam bridge with rail (L) over a stream to a fence stile. Go on uphill to a wall *where you will see a very fine example of a gate pillar with two post slots.* Turn left along the wall and then go through a pillar stile, between walls and turn steeply up right under hawthorn bushes and up two flights of stone steps. At the top turn left to go acutely right round the fence and cross the road in front of the cottages, some four storeys high. Veer left past the end cottage, named Linz, and continue steeply up the signposted footpath between cottages and walls.

At the top with Hill Top Bank (R), zigzag left and right onto a public footpath with a high wall (L) (7km). Carry on until you reach a crag (R): the views from here are the reward for doing the walk this way round; *leftish you can see over to Holme Moss Mast, in the centre up the valley to Meltham and the Mills and on the horizon the road over to Saddleworth, and to the right the V-shaped nick over to Standedge and in the foreground the village of Netherton. To your rear you see a very different view over Huddersfield and beyond, to Newsome, Castle Hill, Emley Mast, Thurstonland Church spire (just peeping over the horizon!) and further round to the right.*

When ready, carry on along the ridge and then follow the woodland path going gently downhill to the far left corner of the wood – don't drop down to the right. The track becomes a short path between gardens and leads to a fence stile onto the road. Immediately follow the wall round to the right between signs 'Sandbeds' (L) and 'Beech Croft' (R). Go into the ginnel between walls turning left and going steeply downhill until you bend left with the path. With a wall (R) carry on down to the kissing gate where you started (8km).

Honley

Honley with its old houses and 'folds' around the church area is worth a visit, including at the bottom of the hill the Coach and Horses, where Luddites drank after murdering a local mill owner.

W4: Thongsbridge

Pillar Stiles

Distance: 5.7km (3½ miles)

Time: 1½ hours

Map: OS Landranger 110 (1:50 000), Explorer 288 (1:25 000)

Parking: on A6024 between Honley and Holmfirth in the vicinity of the Royal Oak on Woodhead Road, grid reference: 147098

Terrain: some stretches of road, field, farm track and path — undulating with the uphill sections early in the walk on either side of Netherthong

Refreshments: the Cricketers Arms in Lower Netherthong

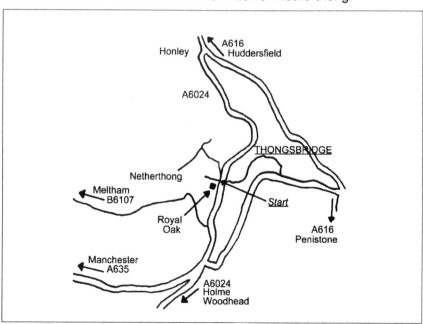

THIS walk is a pleasant stroll up through the outskirts of Netherthong and up and over the fields to the east of Oldfield from where you can gain extensive views of the surrounding countryside. The way back takes you down through pleasant woodland alongside the River Holme. The special feature of the walk is pillar stiles.

On the Woodhead Road (A6024) turn north in the direction of Honley for some 200 metres before veering left up Calf Hill Road. At the end turn left into and up Dean Brook Road. *There is a substantial wall (L) of irregularly shaped stones. About halfway up, as the stream crosses from right to left, there is an old clapper bridge leading to stone steps (L); further up (R) there are two stone water troughs.*

Keep going right up Deanhouse Lane (1km) past the back of cottages, *some with blocked up windows and doors,* and along the wall of former cottages, *now the back of a newly built housing development which blends in well with the old stone style.* At the Cricketers Arms ahead turn right, *and immediately to your right see the "weavers' windows" on the backs of the cottages. Close by was the original site of the first Wesleyan Chapel in the Holme valley and at the far side of the Cricketers Arms car park is the site of the old Huddersfield Workhouse – Deanhouse: what was its origin?* Go on up the lane to a kissing gate beside a wooden farm gate (R) and then to another such combination. Take the line of the wall bending slightly right and then sharper right to a pillar stile. Veer right up to the top of the field to a wall stile left of a telegraph pole.

From here you gain a fine view (R) of Emley Mast and Thurstonland Church peeping over the ridge round to the windmill above Penistone and Woodhead. Walk on diagonally across fields towards Castle Hill in the distance *with a view down over Honley and beyond.* You come to a wall stile and then two pillar stiles on either side of a farm track (2km). Go on to a small gap by a wooden fence leading right to a passage between a fence and wall, and then to a pillar stile. Follow the wall (L) to go through a pillar stile onto the road.

Turn right for 70 metres ignoring a public footpath (L). Just past the red brick Ivy Cottage go left over a wall stile and then diagonally right to an unusual, and difficult to climb, stone stile in the bottom right corner of the field. Follow the line of the wall (L) to two wall

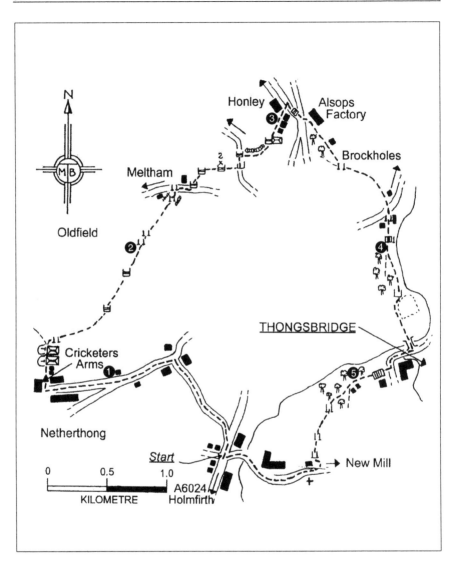

stiles across a gap. Keep along the wall (R) to a gap in the wall. Going
left for 15 metres cross the road and a wall stile (R). Follow the wall
as it bends left, again for Castle Hill to a wall slab stile beside a metal
gate (R). The grass track changes to tarmac, concrete and back to a
tarmac road past bungalows (R). Go between houses to the road at
the bottom (3km).

Mytholm bridge

Turn right for 25 metres and find a path leading to stone steps down left. (If you reach the speed restriction signs, you have gone too far). Cross the roads including the main one. Turn right. Immediately past Allsops' works (L) take a footpath down alongside a wall (L) that lies between the factory drive and the main road. Go through the narrow woodland past stone houses. Go across a field to a broken pillar stile and left down a lane. Follow it as it curves to the road. *The Old Smith Place buildings and bridge are to the left.* Cross the road and go into what looks like a private drive, through a pillar gap beside a farm gate between stone outbuildings and onto a track. Through a metal gate by two short stone pillars enter the pleasant Hagg Wood. Eventually you walk along a terrace above the River Holme (L).

(4km) Take the left-hand fork down the slope keeping close to the river, *with new stylish houses on the opposite bank,* until you go through a gap in the wall. Turn right up the lane and left round past a caravan park, garage and pond (L). At the junction of lanes go straight over onto a track between walls. At the metal Mytholm bridge cross the river and go right into Luke Lane and over the confluence of New Mill Dike and the River Holme. Just after a left bend between Thongs Mill buildings turn right at a footpath sign onto the path, with the mill wall (L), up six steps and on into a wood.

Follow the wall (L) for some way. At a point (5km) where there are two large houses over the wall, one having mock tudor walling, and a stone pillar gateway set in the wall, take the fork down right on a track between holly bushes to a pillar stile out of the wood. Cross two fields via two pillar stiles, *with Thongsbridge Cricket ground (R)*, and turn left onto an unmade lane. Turn right into Miry Lane and passing Thongsbridge Church (L) wind round to the top junction with A6024 and wherever you have parked your car (5.7km).

W5: Netherthong

A thong is just a thong . . . ?

Distance: 6.8km (4¼ miles)

Time: 2 hours

Map: OS Landranger 110 (1:50 000), Explorer 288 (1:25 000)

Parking: in the vicinity of the Cricketers' Arms in Netherthong

Starting Point: the Cricketers' Arms, grid reference: 139009

Terrain: farm tracks, lanes, field paths, and short stretches of road – the walk contains some moderately steep but short ascents, and some stretches of gorse!

Refreshments: the Cricketers' and Clothiers' Arms, both in Netherthong

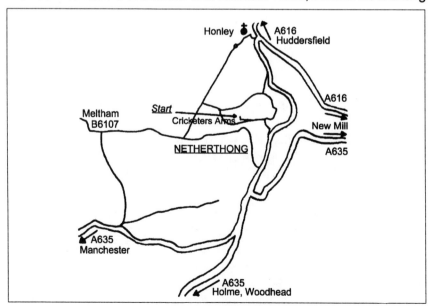

THIS walk takes you up and down a couple of pleasant valleys passing close to or through several very picturesque hamlets,
Netherthong, Upperthong, Wolfstones and Oldfield, all of which
contain fine examples of local architecture dating from 17th century
right up to modern renovations. You can also pause at several places
to gaze at the different and wide panoramic views. What, as far as
place names are concerned, is a Thong?

At the junction of roads with the Cricketers' Arms (R) on the corner,
face southwards and move towards the main village of Netherthong,
veering diagonally right downhill and left to the road junction.
*Glance down left to see the row of modern cottages built tastefully in
keeping with the original style of local buildings.* Turn right for 10
metres, then left up a flight of stone steps and uphill over block setts
until you reach the road at the top. Turn right into School Lane, pass
the Clothiers' Arms and bear left up Church Street, passing the
church (L) *with its large bell above the clock.* After two houses (R), *the
Manor House and Meadow Sweet,* take the lane diagonally down to
the left, where the sign says 'leading to Broomy Lea Lane'.

At the fork keep to the right and carry on until you come to the
end of the row of semi-detached houses (L). The tracks fork left and
right: go straight ahead over a wall stile in the angle of the field opposite. Go diagonally left over the field to another wall stile. Turn left
on a track and continue on between walls (1km) – can be very wet –
and then all the way down to the stream in the bottom. Cross the
stream on stones and go left up the track, following it all the way
round, ignoring any tracks down to the left, until you come to a public footpath (L) with a seat (R), *where you can pause a while to take in
the view down over Holmfirth.* Carry on along Holt Lane and past the
fine mansion, The Holt (R), and straight on up the Hill (2km).

Wind your way round right and left between houses and farm
buildings. Keep going on the track as it winds its way right and left
between walls. Just past Scratchfold Barn and Matlock Farm (R), immediately before getting into Upperthong, *where 'Compo' of The Last
of the Summer Wine is buried,* turn right into Lydgetts on a public
footpath in front of modern houses (L) (3km). *Take the opportunity to
take in the wide view on your right from Castle Hill to the north east,*

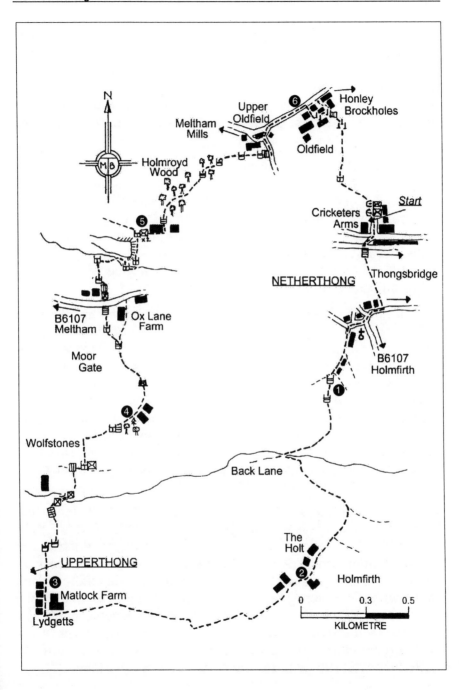

the spire of Thurstonland church and Emley Moor Mast straight ahead, and the modern windmills just peeping over the horizon to the south east. Proceed on into the field keeping the wall (R) and take the wall stile to drop down onto a walled track. Turn right for 50 metres, then left over a wall stile, past two opposing metal gates. The track takes you down stone steps through wooden gates and over a stream.

At this point look upwards to the left to see a large house in a magnificent position high up. The path from here takes you up and round to the left. Through a small wooden gate beside a metal gate turn right for 20 metres before on the left taking a fence stile beside a gate. Go straight uphill alongside a wall (L) and halfway up turn right following a fence along a level stretch before going up left to a fence stile and wall stile, so close that you don't have to touch the ground in between! Then skirt a mixed wood (R) with fir trees alongside the fence and continue to farm buildings (R) (4km).

The farm track takes you up left through a metal gate and between walls over the top into another valley. Before the track bends to the right, take a diagonal wall stile on the left and veer left to the corner of the field where there is a triangular shaped fence stile. Following close by the line of the wall (R), *look around you to see in variously separate locations renovated buildings which display evidence of earlier days of weaving at second or third storey height; in some cases the windows have been blocked up.* Descend a row of stone steps and cross the road; steps up take you on a tarmac and signposted path through a fence gate and a metal gate and round left until you come to a wall stile on the right.

Go down to the fence stile at the bottom-left corner: the arrow points left – but this is the less attractive way via the road (i.e. right up Knoll Lane, then right down a farm lane). A more attractive, but tedious, route is to go right and through the gorse and brambles (!); cross a stream twice as well as two fence stiles at right angles to each other with the stream in between. On your left is a large mound-like structure with a wall and massive buttresses: *is it possible that this was the retaining wall of a 'gathering pond' for use in the erstwhile weaving activities of the nearby cottages?* Head slightly right up the field for a wall stile with two fence gates on its right (5km).

Once in the lane, go straight across and past the stables (R) and in front of the cottages (L), then sharp left by a telegraph pole up a footpath. *In a few metres glance to the right to see a pond nestling behind the cottages.* Go over a wall stile and up past a wooden gate (L) into a copse, over a little causeway and out across an open field. *Again glance down to the right to view a larger pond with its own bridge in the middle (Japanese style?).* A wall stile takes you into a wood and another takes you out again. Further on, cross left over the wall by a stile, and keeping the wall on your right you emerge onto Miry Lane via a wall stile. Turn left uphill and over the top you enter the cluster of old and renovated buildings of Upper Oldfield; *the ones on the left are of particular interest, including a 16th century cruck barn.* The lane bends to the right and you turn right into Oldfield Lane. *As you walk down the road for 250 metres, you gain a fine view to the left over Honley and to Huddersfield.*

Turn right (6km) opposite a telephone kiosk just before you come to a converted single storey building *which once was the Oldfield Church of England National School, founded 1838,* and go up the lane towards and left round a cluster of oldish buildings which formed the original hamlet of Oldfield. Opposite a three-storey building (R) go left through a squeeze pillar wall stile, down between the cottages to another pillar stile beside (R) a metal gate. Go diagonally right across the field to a third pillar stile, then right along the line of the wall (R) and down over the field to a field stile *on the far side of which is a seat in memory of Stanley Alsop, 'The Real Squire of Deanhouse'.*

Keep going diagonally left down the field until you straighten out to a kissing gate beside a wooden farm gate in the corner of the field. This takes you to another kissing gate next to a wooden gate and onto a lane past houses. Just before you get to the last group, *look left to the weavers' windows on the backs of the cottages.* You are now back to the Cricketers' Arms (R) and wherever you parked your car (6.8km).

The first Wesleyan chapel in the Holme valley was built near the Cricketers' Arms, and was visited by Wesley twice. Deanhouse, built on the far side of the car park, was famous or infamous for being the Huddersfield District Workhouse.

W6: Holme

A High Level Walk around the Reservoirs

Distance: 8km (5 miles) or 8.5km with a diversion for a view

Time: 2½ to 3 hours

Map: OS Landranger 110 (1: 50 000), Explorer (1:25 000)

Parking: as appropriate in the village of Holmbridge in the vicinity of The Bridge Tavern, the parish church or the church hall

Starting Point: on A6024, The Bridge Tavern, grid reference:122068. (Alternative starting points at parking areas by Ramsden Reservoir, grid reference: 116055; Digley Reservoir (South), grid reference 109060, or (North), grid reference: 111074)

Terrain: meadow and field, farm track, paths and short stretches of road – after an initial longish and steepish uphill stretch, the walk is easy going on waymarked paths with short dips into valleys

Refreshments: available at various hostelries in Holmbridge or Holme

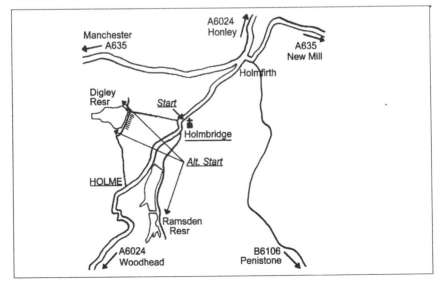

THIS walk involves a substantial uphill pull at its start, but you will be rewarded by splendid extensive views over all the valleys to the north and all the reservoirs that you will visit later. The rest of the walk winds its way at high level attractively around a series of reservoirs, each of which has its own characteristics, and drops you into sheltered valleys before returning you gently back to Holmbridge.

Start the walk along the main road (A6024) towards Holme and past the church of the Shared Parish of St David. Almost immediately, take the road to the left towards Yateholme and in 100 metres bend up right past Fernleigh House Restaurant. At the top of the first rise, after the junction with a road and cottages (L) on Brownhill Lane, take the signposted footpath up the lane to the left. *Note the old sundial high up on the building (L).* Do *not* go left through the houses, but go straight on to the right of the end house of a terrace *with IWI June 14th 1910 above the door – what does IWI stand for?*

    Immediately go through a metal kissing gate on the right of double metal gates, and on through a wooden kissing gate onto a grass track. Go straight on bearing left of the stream to follow the line of the wall (L) up through a narrow wood. At the top of this wood bear right and up the knoll, keeping the gully on your left (1km) until veering diagonally to the right you come to a wall stile beside a metal gate. Turn right onto a grass track between stone walls.

You now have a choice of routes:

To take the more strenous path to gain the extensive view, bend left with the left-hand wall up through a wooden gate and then on up the long track between stone walls to a kissing gate at the highest point of the walk – *the reward! a seat "in loving memory of Jack Gill 1916-1993" for you to take a rest and enjoy the panoramic view to Holme Moss, the reservoirs, to Castle Hill, Emley Mast and beyond.*

Once rested and with your fill of the view, go right and as you go down the track Riding Wood Reservoir will come into view; at the junction turn right downhill until you bend left into the wood.

The gentler route takes you along the wall (R) going straight on slightly downhill through sets of pillars across the field to a fence and then wall stile in front of the wood; join the track straight on into the wood. *Don't miss (L) the remains of stone kilns and the ruined buildings further down the track* before you reach the bottom (2km).

In front of the stone house turn left and then right across the dam wall of Riding Wood Reservoir, *at which point there is a good view of Ramsden Reservoir below right.* The track is now wide and goes up and round between walls until opposite the embankment of Yateholme Reservoir (L) take the footpath right over a wall stile, signposted to Holme and Ramsden. There is a wide gap in the wall and the path turns steeply downhill left to cross the stream by a wooden bridge and then right upwards to a fence stile. Then it bends left (3km) and slightly downhill.

(This walk can be started from the opposite side of Ramsden Reservoir.) Towards the end of the reservoir veer left up to a ladder stile beside a dog gate. *From here is a good view down Brownhill Reservoir.* Take the lower path (R) to a fence stile, cross it and then follow the path left and round the head of a small and picturesque valley. *As you start to descend, look back to view a spur of Brownhill Reservoir and across to Emley Mast on the horizon* (4km).

Cross the stream (Rake Dike) on a stone slab bridge with metal railings. Go up a pebble and cobbled path along a wall (L). At stone pillars veer left up to two wall stiles into and left out of a wood. At a wooden slat gate, take the wall stile (L), turn right and over a fence stile into a lane between a hedge and wall. *Over hedge (L) is the architect designed aptly named 'Underhill House'.* Turn left at the main road and walk into the Square in the hamlet of Holme. Turn right up over stone setts past an arch (L), *dated 1686.* 150 metres up the lane opposite The Nook (L) take a footpath (R) between pillars and a metal gate and on between walls. Go over a fence stile and veer right, away from the wall, to a wall stile in the direction of Digley Reservoir, which you can just see in the far valley (5km).

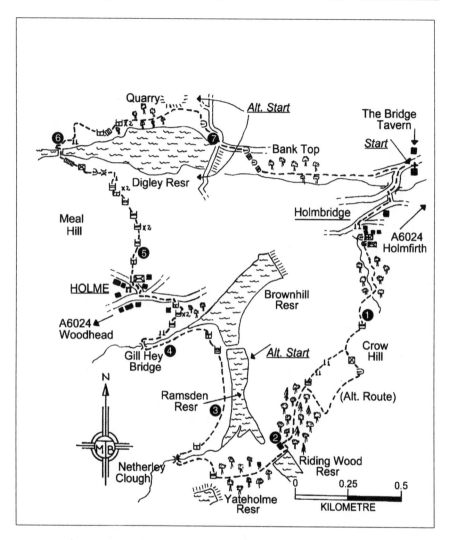

Walk over a succession of fields via four slab stiles. After a fence stile veer right to another slab and fence stile. Heading straight for the reservoir, turn left onto a path over a concrete bridge and a wooden kissing gate. 100 metres further on a gate takes you through a wall (R). The path goes on through a fence gate and down steps to cross the dam wall. Turn left, through a metal gate and right up the track. Pass the seat (L) and go straight on (6km).

Hereabouts you can see the ornamental stone pillars for a house (R), long demolished, and water troughs in the wall (L). The wide track goes down between walls, *further down made of ornamental stones.* The original road went downhill before the reservoir, but now a fence stile takes you along a fence (R). Stone steps take you up onto the foundations of a demolished wall and on to a fence stile. Some steps (R) take you to an uphill track between walls. *The wall (L) contains some weighty stone slabs, no doubt quarried locally at the top of the brow.* Follow the track until just before the end take a footpath through a kissing gate (R), down steps and round to the left to join the main road (7km). (The walk can be started from here, if you park your car on the north or south side of the reservoir.)

Follow the road past the end of the dam wall. As it bends left take a metal kissing gate (R), bear left next to a wall and to steps down onto a path through trees. Go down to another kissing gate, steps and left onto a lane which leads you gently downhill all the way back to wherever you have parked the car (8km).

Holme

This is straggling but charming hamlet of gritstone houses, set in a panoramic landscape of moor and woodland, valleys, reservoirs and farmland. By ancient charter the Graveship of Holme grants free peat to residents, some of whom still burn it, as it is aromatic. The date of 1694 is carved above the Sunday School doorway.

Central Kirklees

Sinister sky over the ruined Hades, its name built proudly in the wall (Walk C5)

C1: Farnley Tyas (A)

To Castle Hill and Back

Distance: 8km (5 miles)

Time: 2½ hours including taking in the view at Castle Hill

Map: OS Landranger 110 (1:50 000), Explorer 288 (1: 25 000)

Parking: somewhere close to the centre of Farnley Tyas, grid reference: 165128

Terrain: meadow and field, farm track, path and short stretches of road – the walk involves two steepish ascents to Castle Hill and back up to Farnley

Refreshments: at the Golden Cock in the centre of Farnley or at Castle Hill Hotel

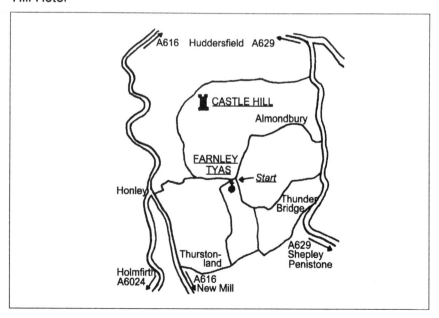

THIS moderately strenuous walk starts from the picturesque village of Farnley Tyas and takes you twice down into the valley between Farnley and Castle Hill. On the way out you get magnificent views of Castle Hill and on the way back you go down into a delightful part of the valley alongside a stream. The panoramic views from Castle Hill are undoubtedly second to none in Kirklees, even in West Yorkshire, and whilst you are up there, do take the opportunity to walk round the embankments and observe their grandeur as well as the size of the enclosure. A special feature of this walk is the number of 'squeeze' stiles made of wooden or stone pillars.

With the Golden Cock in front of you, take the road to the right towards Almondbury (in a NNE direction) for a few metres. Immediately past 2A The Great Barn (L), turn left down a lane between walls. As you come to two metal gates ahead, bend left; as the path drops down to the right, go through the pillar stile ahead. Keep close to the wall/fence (R) downhill to a fence stile. *All along this stretch you gain fine views of the tower on Castle Hill across the valley.* Continue to another fence stile, then a wall stile, and to a pillar stile made of a cut-off telegraph pole with a wall (R). Go over another wall stile and continue straight on over old wall foundations and along the edge of a field. Then you go along the top of the wall which stands proud to the field (R). At the next fence stile (1km) follow the wall and then go over the field to a fence stile in a holly hedge.

Go straight on over a wide track. Under the power pylons take the fence stile on the left over the wall. Go up along the wall and fence (R) until you cross a fence stile to go diagonally right up the field towards a hamlet. A fence stile takes you up a short avenue of fences to squeeze between a stone (L) and wooden (R) pillar. Go up alongside a leylandii hedge (R) to turn right and left in front of the stone houses and on up the tarmac lane at Farnley Hey. Just beyond the last house in the row (R) squeeze right between the wooden pillar and the wall. Having passed beyond the wall, go straight on past a tree (L) and then a small electricity pylon (R) to a fence stile in mid-field. Veer right to pillars in a gap in the wall (2km).

Turn right along the wall to squeeze between stone pillars followed by wooden pillars. Go on to skirt the wood (R) *which conceals quite a deep ravine.* Continuing into a gap, take a fence stile beside the wall (L); follow this wall on until you have to squeeze through wooden pillars beside a metal farm gate. Proceed to the farm buildings; go through the metal gate ahead and turn left up the field following the line of the wall (L) until you cross a fence stile over the wall (3km).

Turn right (not as indicated!) along the wall firstly to a fence stile and then over another fence stile onto the road beside a white cottage, *named 'Ogley'* (R). Turn left up Lumb Lane past the small car park (L) and Hillside (R). Climb the steps on your right and proceed on to the Tower.

The panoramic views from here are truly breathtaking. It would be pointless to try to mention all the sights – there are so many, and the better the weather, the more will come into view to the far horizons in every direction – just take your fill in your own time. If you care to climb the steps of the tower at its north east end to the first corner you will see the following inscription:

The corner stone of this tower erected by public subscription
to commemorate the completion of 60th year of the reign of
Her Majesty Queen Victoria June 20 1897
laid on 25 June 1898 by John Frecheville, son of
Sir John William Ramsden, Bart, Lord of the Manor

Once sated with the view, you may care to walk round the edge of the enclosure, in a clockwise direction past the Hotel, and on to the far end. *This will give you a good idea of its size with ditch and further embankments below – when were they built?* Carry on round the upper embankment to the right until you reach the road (Hillside) (4km).

Turn left into the road and follow it all the way round to the junction with Lumb Lane. Turn left and go downhill to the white cottage. Just beyond it take the wide track to the left; *there is a stone direction sign to Mistal Barn in the wall opposite.* As this track bends left, go through the wall gap (R) and down the stone steps. Follow the wall (L) down to a wooden pillar stile and further down to a fence stile in the left corner. Go through the wall and across the road. Go over a wall stile and head for two standing stones (5km).

Turn right before the stones to follow the hedge (L) until you

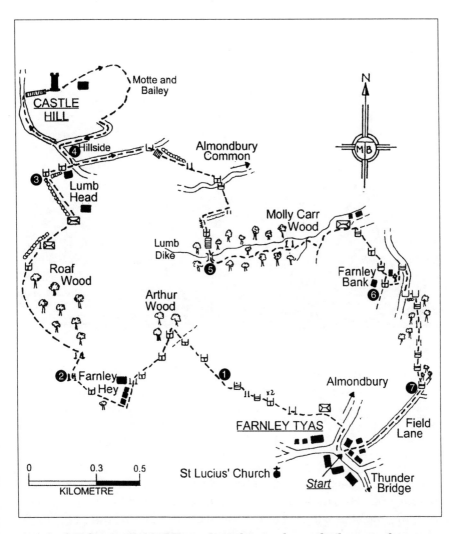

reach the fence. Do NOT go straight on through the gap, but turn
sharp left through the wide gap and follow the fence (R) down to a
fence stile. This takes you into the wood down two flights of stone
steps to planks over the stream. *The walk along this part of the valley
is delightful.* Going left you have a choice of paths depending on the
state of the ground: the lower path follows the stream, winding
around and up and down, even crossing the stream twice, and exits
via a stone pillar stile, but the path can be very muddy; the other

Castle Hill and Farnley Tyas

path goes uphill and then left at a higher level until it drops down, joining the lower path on the left, to cross a stream via stepping stones. Proceed on and through the gap in the hedges to cross another stream. Ggo left of a tumbledown building onto a track bordered by a hawthorn hedge (R) interspersed with wild roses and blackberry.

Go through a metal gate onto a track (6km) ; some 20 metres on, over a fence stile (L) *you can see an old cowshed with wooden beams over the doorways, the left one blocked up with a red brick wall.* Opposite the fence stile is a wall stile (R); go over it and head steeply uphill for a small fence stile in the top corner of the field; it looks to be placed halfway between two houses and has a large holly bush above it. Over the stile continue up left of the bush to the corner of a wall. Just above the corner take a wall stile (R) into a tarmac drive and left up to a wide track.

Turn right up the track between walls. *Note a most unusual weather vane on the gable end of the outhouse down to your right – a builder with a barrow and a pile of mortar, putting the last stone in the archway!* You come to a fence stile with farm gates on either side, wooden (L) and metal (R). Over the stile, don't go straight on, as indicated, but turn left at a right angle and go uphill left of spoil heaps to the trees and wall at the top of the slope. Turn left and go through the trees/bushes under the line of electric cables and just past the line telephone wires to a wall stile (R). Over the wall stile, turn right and walk along the road (take care as traffic moves quickly on this stretch) for 200 metres. Cross and go left through the wall gap and up along the wall (R). Halfway up go right through a wall gap, then diagonally left up to a zigzag stile through the wall (7km).

Veer right up round a holly bush through mixed woodland to exit at the top of the slope through stone pillars. Go diagonally over the crest of the field to stone pillars through a wall. *Take in the view left over the valley to Emley Mast.* Continue diagonally left across two fields and two wall stiles to bend left with the wood and over a wall stile with a metal gate (R). Turn right onto the farm track and go on up between walls until you pass Sycamore Farm and Barn (R) to come out opposite the Golden Cock, and to wherever you have parked your car (8km).

C2: Farnley Tyas (B)

Holme Valley Views

Distance: 3.6km (2¼ miles)

Time: 1 hour

Map: OS Landranger 110 (1:50 000), Explorer 288 (1: 25 000)

Parking: at the entrance to Dartmouth Recreation Ground on Butts Lane, south west of the centre of the village of Farnley Tyas, grid reference: 162126

Terrain: meadow and field, farm track, path and short stretches of road – generally level ground with one moderate descent and one ascent

Refreshments: at the Golden Cock in the centre of Farnley Tyas

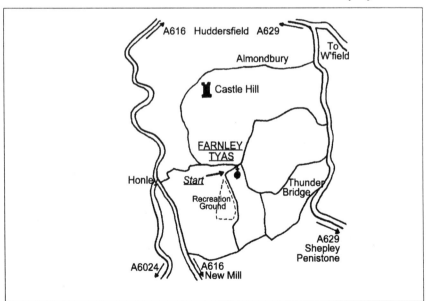

THIS walk is a gentle stroll for an hour or so starting and finishing near the attractive village of Farnley Tyas. The particular feature is that halfway round you gain excellent panoramic views across the Holme valley and to the distant hills.

The Dartmouth Recreation Ground has a plaque, *which commemorates its gift to Thurstonland and Farnley Tyas by Rt. Hon. William Heneage, 6th Earl of Dartmouth, to be used as a public plea-sure ground for the purpose of cricket, football or other games (1927).* Enter the Ground through widely spaced gate-posts and follow the wall (R) ignoring the paths through it (R). Go up through two stone pillars, then squeeze between a metal gate (L) and wall (R), and past a large slab stile with a metal gate (R), and up between walls to the road. Turn right and past Ivy Farm (L).

At the next lane turn right into it and down between the walls with the wood (R). In parts you walk over cobbled setts, *suggesting it is an old trackway (1km)*. After going downhill and round to the left, you increasingly gain a panoramic view *across the valley to Netherthong and Honley, and in the further distance to Longley Farm (L), Holme Moss, West Nab and Standedge, a glimpse of M62, the windmills above Halifax, and round to Castle Hill (R)*. Follow the track round passing a farm (R), and then down to the farm at the bot-tom through two wooden gates.

Turn left and to a fence stile between a gate (L) and a holly bush (R). Follow the wall round right to a fence stile, then left round a wall (L) to go between stone pillars. *Downhill (L) is a former mill pond, now for private fishing.* Turn right round a wall (R), cross a couple of trickling streams (2km) and continue onto a flagged path following the line of the wall. Go uphill to a fence stile over a wall. Follow the wall (R) and then go through a gap to follow a wall (L) *with a wooded glade down below*. Go to a zigzag fence stile, cross a stream and go up stone steps. Continue through another zigzag fence stile to bear left along a wall (L) and up to a wall and fence stile in the top left corner.

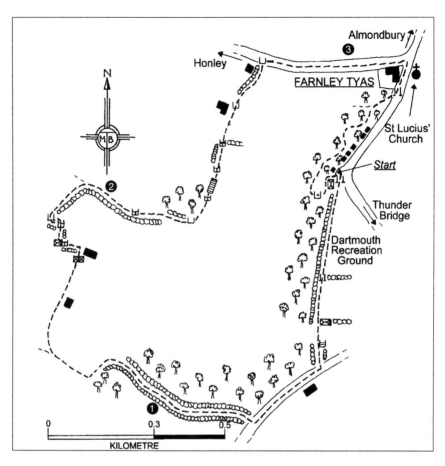

Carry on up the field along a wall (L) and past farm buildings to squeeze through the wall gap and walk over slabs, bending right and left round the wall to exit through a wall gap. Cross the road and go right uphill. (3km) At the Farnley Tyas sign cross the road again to the right-hand pavement and go up past the CE(C) First School (R). Turn right into Butts Lane. Just past the school entrance (R) go right through gateposts and onto a track through woodland. Go over a concrete base and round a circular dip – *it has a thick stone wall surround – for what purpose?* Carry on along the backs of houses (L), until after the last one veer left, over a wall and acutely back to squeeze between a metal gate (L) and wall (R) to your car (3.6km).

C3: Thunder Bridge

Woodlands and Weather Vanes

Distance: 8.7km (5½ miles)

Time: 2½ hours

Map: OS Landranger 110 (1:50 000), Explorer 288 (1: 25 000)

Parking: at a lay-by on Grange Lane (off Birks Road) up from Thunder Bridge to Farnley Tyas halfway through Boothroyd Wood, locally known as Hospital Wood, grid reference: 183118. *Why is it known as Hospital Wood?*

Terrain: meadow and field, woodland, farm track, path and short stretches of road – the walk is undulating with moderate ascents and descents

Refreshments: at The Woodman, Thunder Bridge; the Rising Sun on A629, Shelley

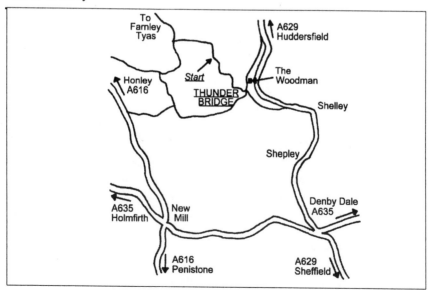

THIS very pleasant and relatively easy walk encircles the aptly named Thunder Bridge, crosses the Dike which gives it its name, climbs up and over close to Kirkburton, skirts Shepley, Stocksmoor and Thurstonland, and halfway round crosses the Huddersfield-Penistone railway. The walk also takes you through several stretches of very picturesque woodland and there are lots of 'points of interest' to see and enjoy.

Start off in a slightly north of east direction by going through stone pillars alongside mixed woodland (L) and a wall (R). *Look across to your right to see Shelley in the distance through a break in the woods* . At crosspaths carry straight on through the trees, following the path

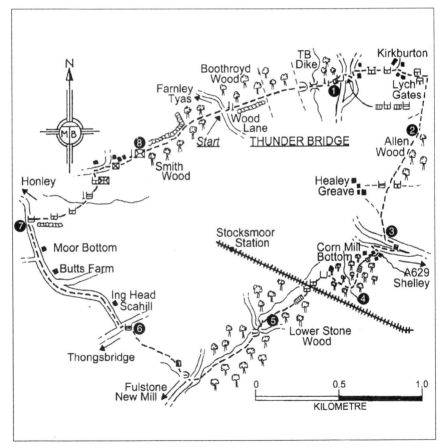

as it goes steeply downhill, across a short stretch of open ground *(a protected meadow)* to a metal kissing gate and a wooden bridge with metal rails over the Thunder Bridge Dike. Veer diagonally left uphill. A stone pillar stile takes you into a wood and the path winds over two or three little brooks. Stone steps take you up to a hole in the wall (1km).

Take care and listen: this is the main road to Huddersfield and there is a blind bend (R). Cross the road to go up stone steps, over a fence stile and up along a wall (L). Go up the field to stone steps and a wall stile. Veer right up a short path. At the road turn left for 40 metres. *On the house (L) is a weather vane with a cock with a long neck!* Immediately past the house Overdale (R) turn right into a ginnel enclosed by a fence (R) and overgrown wall (L). At the end go over a fence stile between stone posts. Go straight on keeping to the right of the wall in the direction of Emley Mast. Come to a fence stile beside two very solid gate pillars with a blocked-up gate, and continue on between walls. *As you near the village of Kirkburton, you can see the church spire and cricket ground away to your left.*

As the track bends left, go right up between Low Town cottages and Yew Tree Barn (L) *with a weather vane of three ducks.* As you progress along the lane you go between two wooden lych-gates leading to graveyards: *the right-hand gate in memory of several members of the Phipps family, including the vicar of 1901-13, has ornate*

Lych-gates, Kirkburton

ironwork; the left-hand one is in memory of Harriet Shaw. At the T-junction turn right and take the path to the right of the paved drive ahead. This path goes up between trees (R) and a hedge/fence (L), and then is paved with stone slabs (2km).

Carry on up an increasing incline between variously trees and walls. Just before you crest the hill, *look over the fields to the right to see all the way down the valley to Waterloo, the chimneys of Zeneca, Bradley and the hills beyond.* Over the crest of the hill, *you get a good view over to Castle Hill (far right), Stocksmoor and Thurstonland, and in the far distance to Holme Moss and the windmill at Longley Farm.* Ignore the fence stile (L) and wall stile (R), *but a house (R) in the Healey Croft complex (R) has two weather vanes with gundogs.* Carry on to join a tarmac lane which takes you down to the main road (3km).

Turn left and enter the 30 mph area of Shelley. Cross the road and before the first building (R), take the stone steps down on to a path between walls. At the bottom turn right into the road and down past cottages (L). *Note no. 20 (R), the Weavers' House with its typical windows at first and second storeys.* Just past the period residence (L), Bank House, turn left onto a public bridleway (Long Lane), which takes you right over the stream at Corn Mill Bottom. *There is an imposing gate pillar to Millwood House (L) and a dovecote window (possibly overgrown with ivy) on the end of Barn Cottage (R) with a dog weather vane on its far end.* Turn left up a cobbled path between walls. In 60 metres take two stone steps up right and follow a path round to the left into the wood and further on up more stone steps.

(4km) Continue on for some 150 metres and at a fork take the path which goes down right to the stream; cross it and bear right uphill taking either fork of the path, as they join up further on. Proceed to go through a hole in the wall. Turn left up the path winding round to two fence gates on either side of the Penistone – Huddersfield railway; take care – *Shepley station is to the left and Stocksmoor to the right.* Having crossed, immediately take the flight of wooden steps down to the right. *At the bottom note the stream culverted into a tunnel through the embankment.* Bend with the path up left following the line of the stream in the bottom (R). *Further up, where the stream meanders, its shale banks are clear to see.* Eventually stone steps take you through a V-shaped hole in the wall into Field Way where there is a seat (5km).

Cross the road to a fence kissing gate (L). Keep to the main path, slightly uphill and bend round to cross a trickle. Continue on for 150 metres and as you near the stream, *note its stone slab bed.* Where steps come down from the left, cross the stream on stepping stones and go up through a fence kissing gate. Cross the road and, left and right, up a footpath to go over a wall and through a metal gate. Follow the line of the fence and stream (L) uphill until you come at the top of the field to a wall stile taking you into Stocks Lane (6km).

Turn left and then right into Ing Head Lane. After passing Scahill buildings (R) at the bend of the road *you will come to an animal (cat/dog) cemetery (R).* At the junction with Stocks Moor Road *on the right there is an old trapezoidal stone signpost with on two sides directions to Shepley, Holmfirth, Fulstone, Farnley and Shelly (sic!).* Go over into Browns Knoll Road, *passing Butts Farm, Top O' Th' Lane (R).* As the road (Town Moor) bends left to Thurstonland and its church, go straight on towards Farnley. As you go up the next rise, *to your right you can see the ventilation shaft to the railway.*

(7km) As the road begins to descend, take the footpath right over a wall stile with wooden planks and go along the wall (R). *You gain a fine view of Emley Mast.* Veering slightly left, you take two fence stiles through walls; after the second you descend and cross the stream. Go on up past a gorse bush (L) to a wall stile (with jutting stones and an old pillar on its left). Go up to a fence stile beside a wooden farm gate (R), and straight on up the lane to the main road. Turn right, passing Rose and Meadow Cottages (L), and as it bends left, take the footpath right past new houses (L), and go through a fence gate along a wall (L). *The house on the end of the row has a horse weather vane, and the furthest house has a colonnade with arches.* Go between stone pillars with a wooden gate on the right, and on into a variegated wood (8km). *There is an exceptionally well-built stone wall on your left.* Return to wherever you have parked your car (8.75km).

C4: Wooldale and Scholes

The Two Villages

Distance: 5km (approx. 3 miles)

Time: 1½ hours

Map: OS Landranger 110 (1:50 000), Explorer 288 (1: 25 000)

Parking: as appropriate in the village of Wooldale, close to the Wooldale Arms

Starting Point: Wooldale Arms, grid reference:153089

Terrain: meadow and field, farm track, lane, paths and short stretches of road

Refreshments: of the liquid kind can be obtained at the Wooldale Arms, and The Boot and Shoe, Scholes

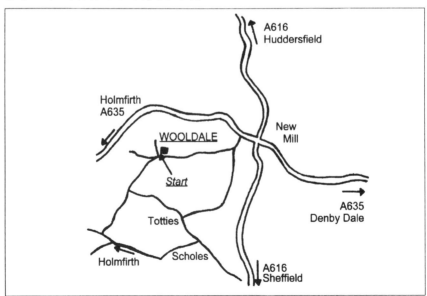

THIS walk is a gentle stroll taking in two typically picturesque West Yorkshire stone villages which are increasingly seeing cottage conversions and more modern house developments. After an initial descent the way is moderately uphill, but after a mill quite steep up from the river to Scholes. From there on it is gentle and the descent back into Wooldale affords good views over Holmfirth and Thongsbridge.

With the Wooldale Arms at your back, take the road south east towards Totties and Scholes for some 50 metres. At the first corner bear left down over cobbles, *taking note of the two stone fountains with brass spout on your right.* Going left of the metal gate between stone pillars, take the path downhill and round to the right, but not too far – opposite the stone cottage (R) turn left down a narrow avenue of hedges with tumbledown buildings on your right. At the junction of paths go straight over and between hedges (can be muddy), through two sets of metal barriers, over a stream. Keep straight on.

Skirt houses (L) and go up the field, in, above and out of a playground area towards the far top corner of the field. Follow

Cottages at Wooldale

the path on the level: at a stone pillar (L) before you reach the fence ahead, turn right up through the allotments until you are level with New Mill church (in mid distance left) i.e. about two-thirds up the allotments. Turn left and the wall stile right in front of you will take you along a wall (L) to two wooden stiles next to the cottage (1km). Over them turn right to the wall stile by the yard gate, and down the lane to the road.

Turn right up the road for 50 metres, ignoring the sign to the left, and follow the wall (L) down a flagged path and through the stone pillars beside a metal gate. The path, sometimes muddy, follows a terrace between bushes. *100 metres on your right there is a good example of a stone gatepost with wooden slot holes.* The river and a waterfall can be seen down on your left.

Take a fence stile into the wood and a track joins your path from uphill right. Continue on between low walls *covered in moss and lichen.* At the mill bear right steeply uphill on a path which halfway up contains cobble sets. Near the top, steps lead you to a wooden pole stile (R); the path goes over the brow between the trees and up the field, following the wall (L) to a wall stile (2km) and left into a lane between walls, *containing some large dressed slabs.* At the main road the Boot and Shoe is 150 metres to the left in the centre of the village of Scholes.

Go straight over the road and up between the cottages: *there are some fine old buildings in this settlement* as you zig left and right, and up the track past an old barn (L) to a modern house at the top; bending left and right you come out into Mount Scar View. Turn right into Cherry Tree Walk and then within a few metres turn first left into Ryefields (unnamed); take the ginnel opposite no. 66 and on the left-hand side of no. 60 through the stone stile, across the field and over a succession of stone stiles – *one of these is of the pillar kind, and several show severe wear and tear from all the feet that have used them over time.* Eventually veer right and then left across three fields *– in the last two you may see the path slightly proud to the surrounding land with a shallow drain on the left side – why is this so?* (3km).

Turn left into the lane and right at the junction. Go past Shaley House and The Channery, and take the right fork into Stake Lane

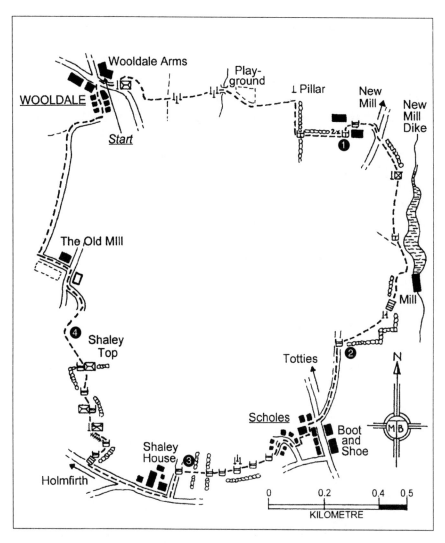

Bank. *From here you gain a wide and fine vista to the windmill above Longley Farm round to Holme Moss above Arrunden and Holmfirth.* Soon you will come on your right to a flight of steps up to a wall stile and into a field. Follow the wall along (R) heading for Emley Mast in the distance to a wall stile. Over this and at the end of the field squeeze through between the wall and the fence end, and turn left onto the farm track. Again squeeze between the fence (L) and a wooden gate to go over a wall stile, right of a metal gate. Continue on and over the next wall stone, veer right walking in the direction of Castle Hill in the distance to a wall stile which is on the left-hand side of another metal gate, level with the corner of the wood away to your right.

From that point on you walk along a track between two walls; at the end of the straight, on the corner, you get a fine view over Holmfirth, Wooldale, and Thongsbridge (4km). Follow the track round to turn right into the road; round the corner turn left up the lane past The Old Mill. *On the left is a stone trough and on the garage (R) a weather vane with 1986 on it; over the wall on the left is a village football pitch, floodlit, no less!* At the junction turn right down the lane which eventually narrows, bearing right between the walls and exit amongst cottages. Turn left down into South Street: *on your right is a long thin tapering three-storey building with Thimble Cottage on the end.* At the bottom return to wherever you have parked your car (5km).

C5: Holme Styes

Uplands and Lowlands

Distance: 11km (7 miles)

Time: 3 hours

Map: OS Landranger 110 (1: 50 000), Explorer 288 (1: 25 000)

Parking: as appropriate in the village of Hepworth near The Butcher's Arms

Starting Point: The Butcher's Arms, grid reference: 163068

Terrain: meadow and field, farm tracks, paths and short stretches of road – the walk is moderate, but also has a few steep descents and ascents, including finally back up to Hepworth

Refreshments: available at The Butcher's Arms all day (Saturdays and Sundays), over lunchtime on Fridays, every evening 6-11pm

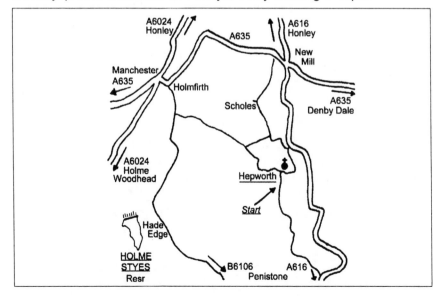

THIS longish walk contains lots of sights and views that will delight you. It takes you gently and steadily 'upland' onto the ridge above Hepworth and Hade Edge, before skirting the forest that overlooks Holme Styes Reservoir, and then dropping you down into the Arrunden valley. It returns by climbing above Longley to afford you magnificent panoramic views in all directions. The final stretch takes you down a picturesque mini-gorge before returning you to Hepworth. The walk takes you past many stone cottages and former 'home' weaving buildings, typical of this part of West Yorkshire.

Facing south and with your back to The Butcher's Arms, walk 15 metres before going right up a footpath between walls and fences and over two stone stiles. Over the wall stile go straight ahead up the field through a gate, continuing on under the wires between pylons and through an open gate in the wall. As the path bends right in the middle of the field, go straight on to the wall stile beside the sheep hole (1km). Continue straight ahead to the wall stile beside a metal gate (R).

Turn right into the lane. As you move on after Dean Lane, *you can see a stone spring in the field (R), and across the valley a good example of the 'home' weaving buildings - the third storey windows are the sure indication! After a metal gate down in the wood to your right you can see a well-built stone footbridge over a stream, and immediately on your left on the roadside a stone trough set in the wall.* After Upper House Road, take the two fence stiles in quick succession on your left (2km), and then follow the wall (L) over two more fence stiles and to a wall stile in mid-fence. Cross the next field to a metal farm gate out onto the road.

Cross the road (B6106) and, slightly to the right, take the wall stile and go up the left-hand side of the field. In 100 metres, turn right for 50 metres along a wall, then left over a wall stile. Follow the wall and fence round to go through a metal farm gate at the left corner; cross the track and the wall stile into the far field to follow the wall (L) as it sweeps round right. *This wall, as others hereabouts, is extremely well constructed with dressed stones and equal-sized copings.* The path ends at the lane. Turn left (3km) and walk increasingly uphill and past Snittlegate Farm (L) until you reach Flight Hill. *What is a Snittle*

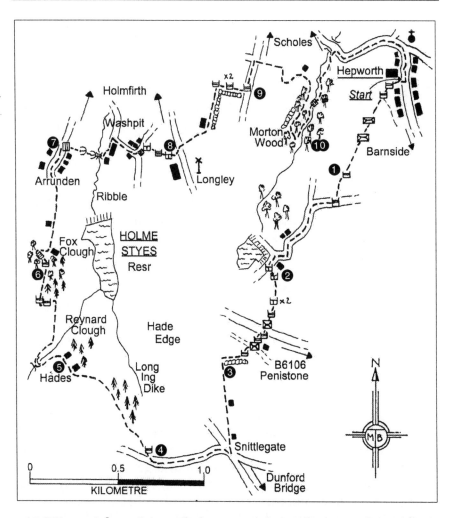

gate? Turn right, not acutely but at a right angle, onto a lane which takes you close to the top of the ridge. *From a seat (R) you can enjoy the extensive panoramic view all the way round from Holme Moss to Castle Hill and Emley Moor Mast.*

Beyond a bridleway (L) (4km) and trees (R), as the road bends right take the forest track down to the right over a stone stile with gate (R). At a junction to the right carry straight on into the dip *with a seat and pool (L)* and up past a renovated building (Woodland Management and Training), and two ruined buildings further on – *the* name *Hades is spelled out (proudly) in the stones of the wall beyond* (5km). *Elysium is not far away – what are the classical allusions of Hades and Elysium?*

The track now goes round down left, across a stream and up right in a long sweeping curve. Following the track round you come to a junction; turn left and in 80 metres go over a wall stile beside a metal gate (R); turn immediately right to go over another wall stile and down the field with a wall (R). At the far end take care in crossing the wall stile and taking the steps downhill (6km).

Go down left to cross the stream on stepping stones and turn acutely back up to the derelict buildings, taking the track on their left-hand side. As you go straight on past a lane and cottage (L), *look down to your far right to glimpse the head of Holme Styes Dam.* The track, which can be muddy, takes you downhill, round the corner and past a group of houses in the hamlet of Arrunden. Immediately after the last one (7km), take a footpath on the right through a single metal gate, down alongside the wall (L) to a metal kissing gate between stone slabs and further on to a C-bend metal gate and a stone bridge over a stream.

Go left up round the wall and left on to a driveway and out into a road past a row of splendid weavers' cottages. *Further down the road you can see Washpit Mill and dam.* Turn right up the hill (Choppards Lane) between walls *and near the top stop to look at the stone trough in the wall side (R).* At the junction with Cote Road turn left and in 30 metres take the steps up and over a fence stile; going up the field bear right to more steps and a fence ladder stile, along a wall (R) beside Longley Farm to another fence stile. At the end of a fenced-in path take the wooden farm gate on the left into the lane that leads round into the road. Turn left *and you will see rows of large slabs in the foundation of the main road straight up ahead, as well as the windmill on the horizon above.*

At the junction with the main road (8km) go straight over onto a wide and well-made track uphill between walls. *The view from the top is stupendous and breathtaking, a panorama from Holme Moss around the Pennines to Huddersfield, Halifax and on a clear day to Oxenden Moor wind power station on the horizon towards Keighley,* round to Castle Hill, Emley Moor Mast and Birds Edge. Also at the top glance right to look at the rounded corner of the high wall, in itself extremely well-built, again with dressed stone.

Bear left past the cottages down the track between walls. Just beyond a metal gate, a zigzag stone stile takes you into the field on the right along the wall to three wall stiles. Turn left into the road (9km) and walk into the Scholes boundary; take the first lane on the right down to Square Field. At the junction turn right and follow the road round, *noticing that the walls on opposite sides of the road are very differently built.* Go round until just before it bends left down to the farm, go through the gate/gap on the right and follow the wall round (R) – *note how in places it is built of large irregular blocks.* Go through the gap in the wall into Morton Wood – said on the notice to be PRIVATE, but there is a path which turns right keeping you close to the wall and up over the brow of a hill until another wall forces you to turn left downhill very steeply.

At the stream (10km) walk left alongside it down a mini-gorge, firstly on the left and then after stepping stones on the right. *This is a superbly picturesque end to the walk with the cliffs, ferns and mini waterfalls.* A fence stile and track leads you on to the main road which takes you steeply right and left uphill. As you round the corner into Town Gate *with Solomon's Temple on your left, topside of the church,* you can return to wherever you have parked your car (11km).

C6: Hepworth and Barnside

The Walk of the Streams

Distance: 4km (2½ miles)

Time: 1¼ hours

Map: OS Landranger 110 (1:50 000), Explorer 288 (1: 25 000)

Parking: in the vicinity of The Butchers Arms, Hepworth

Starting Point: The Butchers Arms, grid reference: 163067

Terrain: meadow and field, farm track, lane, paths and short stretches of road

Refreshments: available at The Butchers Arms all day (Saturdays and Sundays), over lunchtime on Fridays, every evening 6-11pm

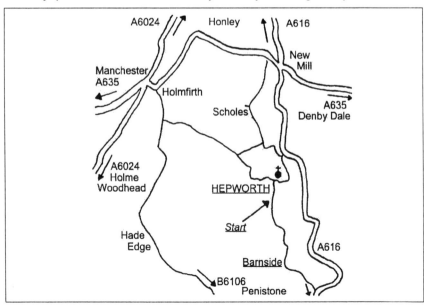

THIS short walk starts at the picturesque stone village of Hepworth, and takes you up and down the nearby hills, crossing a succession of streams. At its highest point you pass within sight of the derelict buildings of Ox Lee and then through the hamlet of Barnside with its renovated cottages. The path is moderately uphill and after Barnside descends into Raikes Dike, from which there is a final steep climb back into Hepworth. For what incident was Hepworth famous (or infamous)?

Start facing south with your back to The Butchers Arms and walk for 50 metres before turning right up Barracks Fold. *Immediately on the right is an old building with wooden and stone lintels over the doors, one of them bearing the date 1791. As you move on between the cottages, note the blocked up windows and doorways, especially on the last building on the left, with the interesting name of Tigh Crosta.* Go up between the walls into Mugup Lane past the backs of houses (L).

At the junction with the main road go straight over onto the track known as Far Field Lane. Go over the broken wall stile at the end (1km) and veer right across the field to the corner by a wall (L). A fence stile takes you down stone steps to a stone bridge over a stream – *a charming spot* – and then up over a fence stile. Take the path to the right, and after another fence stile bear slightly left uphill and round the edge of the knoll, keeping a tributary of the stream on your right. Round the corner you will have a wall on your left: go on up through the trees and the broken down wall heading for twin electricity pylons, *beyond which you can see the deserted buildings of Ox Lee.*

Before reaching the pylons, turn left at right angles, but then veer diagonally left towards a copse of trees and a marker post – the hamlet of Barnside is snuggling in the hollow directly below. Keep to the left of the copse until you reach a wall stile. Having crossed this, go right down the line of the wall (R). Take the stepping stones over another stream and go left down the side of a wall (2km) until you come to a fence stile at right angles at the end of the field. You are now in the hamlet of Barnside.

Turn right up Barnside Lane past several renovated houses (L). After 150 metres turn left into Snug Lane. Continue straight down

Cottages, Hepworth

the lane through the wide fence gate of Upper Barnside Farm, and on the broad track between the walls. At the bottom go over a metal ladder stile, and after two stable boxes (L), go through the fence gate on the left and down through a metal gate to what appears to be a wide bridge. *Do take the time to pause here and look over the side both to the left and right. You may be surprised to see that it is not a bridge as such; to the left you will see the stream disappear into the far side of the rock wall, and on the right you will see it emerge from a shale cavern – quite a remarkable sight in an idyllic spot!* Continue on over the metal ladder stile beside a metal gate. The path takes you on until you go through a wooden farm gate onto the road (3km).

Turn right down the road. *Soon on the left is a seat should you want to rest a while.* Carry on down the road, crossing the stream which runs through the woods on the right until you come to Foster Place Lane on your right. Turn into this and cross the bridge, then go left and through a metal pole stile. The path takes you through the trees to the right of the stream along Raikes Dike. *Note the slabs of bedrock in the stream. You also get a fine view of the backs of houses,*

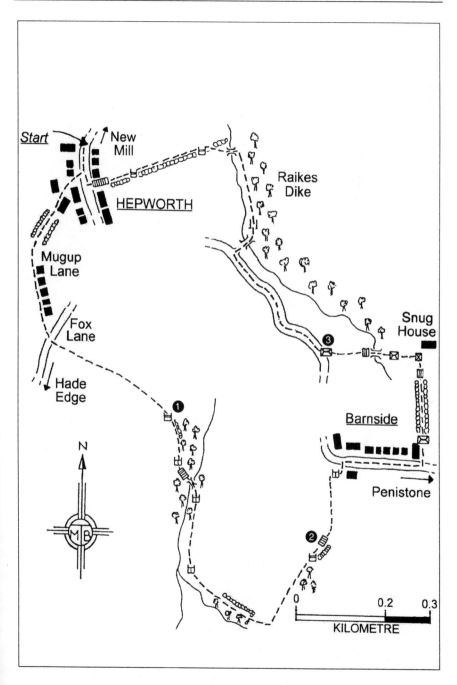

some of them four storeys high, up in Hepworth on the hillside to the left. Before long you need to cross the stream (L) on a wooden bridge and veer up right to a wall stile. Then follow the line of the wall (L) up an increasingly steep incline, at first on a path of paved slabs to a wall stile and finally up several flights of steps. At the top you come out on to the main road. Turn right and return to wherever you have parked your car (4km).

East Kirklees

The Summer House at Cannon Hall (Walk E9)

E1: Briestfield

The Beacon and the Temple

Distance: 9.4km (5¾ miles) – further if you take the 'Beacon' detour

Time: 3 hours – more with the detour

Map: OS Landranger 110 (1: 50 000), Explorer 288 (1: 25 000)

Parking: as appropriate close to the village of Briestfield in the vicinity of the Shoulder of Mutton

Starting Point: Shoulder of Mutton, grid reference: 233175

Terrain: field, farm track, paths and short stretches of road – the walk is undulating with moderately steep ascents and descents

Refreshments: food available at Shoulder of Mutton, Briestfield; The Woolpack, Whitley; and, Hare and Hounds (B6118)

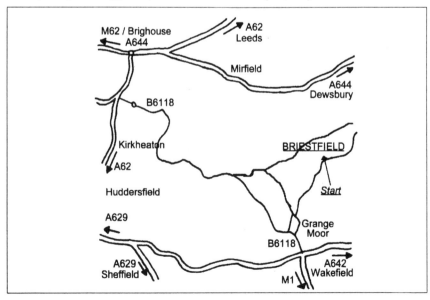

THIS walk starts and finishes in the quiet and attractive village of Briestfield and circles the hamlet of Whitley Lower. There is a number of moderate ascents, but your efforts will be well rewarded at various points with magnificent panoramic views to the north, west and even south. Enjoying these views may extend your walking time!

Starting with the Shoulder of Mutton on your right, walk a few metres to a junction and turn right up the road. 100 metres up this road after passing an old-fashioned telephone box and cottage (R) *with a horse weather vane*, take the public footpath over a wall stile (L). Past the farm buildings zigzag left and right to a wall stile and then on to two more such stiles (the second on a wall end), before going straight up the middle of the field in a westerly direction. You will see coming into view Emley Mast (L) and Whitley Church (R). Over the rise make for the wooden gate in the wall. Across the road and a fence stile, follow the rightish bend of the trees (L) past two posts and to the right of the bush hedge.

The path ahead is indistinct, but make for a stile in the fence diagonally to your right (1km); once at it and with a good view of the church, don't go over the stile but follow the fence along the field all the way until you come to a fence stile in the corner by a hawthorn hedge. Go over it to standing stones in front of a fence stile. Turn right down to and through the farm gate. *The barn (R) is made of a patchwork of wooden doors, etc.* Turn left between the buildings of Clock Royd Farm. Turn right at the main road going down past Pendle Hill Grange (L). At the bottom turn left over the stream and go up a farm track right of the farm buildings and through wooden posts with a metal gate (L). Carry on alongside a stream down in the trees (L) and up to and through the gap ahead (2km).

A signpost points you to the right corner of the field. *As you walk to this corner look at the view over to the power stations in the far distance (R).* At the junction of hedges turn left up the field and under the pylons until you reach the wall stile at the top. Follow the track left all the way round to the main road at the top. Turn right and cross the road for 120 metres. Take the footpath over the wall stile (L) and straight on up through the new plantation before veering diago-

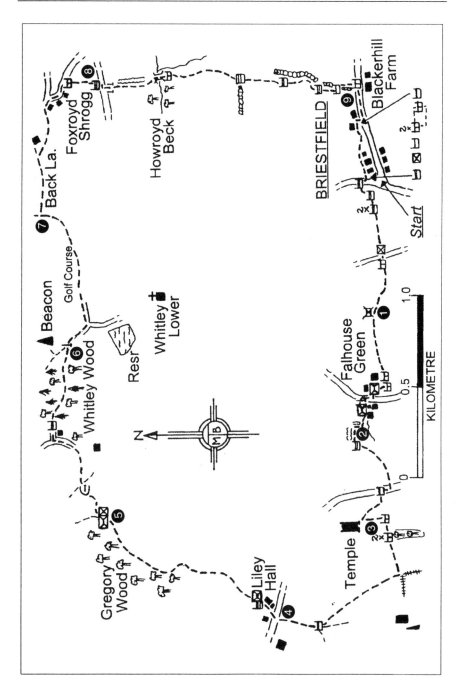

The Temple

nally right to the monument (3km). *Once there a whole new vista of breathtaking proportions meets your eyes to the north, west and even south – beyond the Pennines, Halifax, Bradford and to Leeds can be easily seen on a clear day.*

The monument is called the Temple (built by whom?) and you will see why from its construction. Once you have taken your fill of the view, turn at right angles left towards the fence enclosing a copse of variegated trees. A little way along is a fence stile leading down to others on either side of the cross track. Go straight down to the top right corner of a fence enclosing the field of a large farm beyond. Turn right there and go onto a well-defined footpath to join the lane at a wall stile. Proceed up the lane to the main road (B6118) (4km).

Veer right across the road to go down a public bridleway and between the farm buildings. *Opposite Liley Hall are stone steps leading to an old stile (L), now fenced off.* Carry on down the track past a ladder stile with a metal gate (R). *This track is "The Priest's Path" from Dewsbury to Kirkburton and Almondbury*; halfway down it, over a metal gate, you get a good view of St Mary's Church, Mirfield. Wind your way down over a cobbled track beside the wood (L) to a small wooden gate beside a metal gate (L) at the bottom (5km).

Go through the fence gate and veer right into the dip over the stream and up the path to a wooden kissing gate *with stone gateposts shaped like arrow heads.* Head for the tarmac public bridleway, taking neither of the other footpaths. Bend round over the cattle grid beside an old spreading oak, and you may glimpse the roofs of Camborne Fabrics textile mills down beyond the trees. *Shortly, going up right, is a cobbled track.* Just further beyond at a fork in the road, turn right up the lane past the Registered Office of Hopton Estates (R), *with its rooster weather vane on top and clock on the shed (L).* A wall stile beside a wooden gate (L) takes you into Whitley Wood, of mixed deciduous and coniferous trees, and up the steep path. Near the top there is stone edge paving and you pass a solitary large stone gatepost *with post slots on its further side* (6km).

At the top the Beacon (or Pinnacle) is away to the left – on the golf course! *It is at your own risk from golf ball injury that you make your way to the Beacon; you may think the vastly extensive view is worth the risk, though you can gain virtually the same view from further along the walk. The original Beacon was erected for the Armada victory, but now incorporates a drinking fountain commemorating the centenary in 1991 of Dewsbury District Golf Club.*

To continue the route, at the top of Whitley Wood turn right onto a gravelled path between hedges which is on the Kirklees Way. At the road that comes in from the right, take the left-hand path onto the tarmac public bridleway which then becomes an unsurfaced track with a stone flagged causeway alongside the golf course. *Pause beside the last green (L) to take a last look over to St Mary's Church, Mirfield, the green roof of the College of the Resurrection with M62 motorway and Brighouse further beyond.* After a downhill stretch opposite a holly bush take the path to the right (7km). Your route goes straight on and eventually veers right up a double paved track. At the road junction, take a last look at the view before turning right onto the road. In 120 metres take the footpath over a fence stile (R) and go down the field to a wall stile (8km).

Turn right for 40 metres crossing the road, then left down stone steps and through a wooden three-pillar stile into the field. Go right of the hedge down to a ladder fence stile. Do *not* go over a fence stile (L). At the bottom take the wooden bridge over the meandering Howroyd Beck and immediately a fence stile. Go uphill past standing stones (of an old stile?). Take a line, indistinct at first, up the field keeping the stream down on your left and pass stone steps over a tumbledown wall. You should keep close to the wall on left, going round the corners of the wall to a stone step stile. After a kink in the fence you come to a similar stile. Go up the field with the wall on your left until halfway up you need to cross a stone stile with metal bar to continue on the left side of the wall. Go up to the fence stile opposite Fisherwraithe and Wilson House Farms. Turn right for 160 metres and having passed the white cottage, take the footpath to the right (9km).

There now follows a fascinating stretch of the route, which is the 'pièce de resistance'! Believe it or not, you now have to walk up to the house ahead, go left across the front of the house, and over a stone and then a fence stile. Next, you cross diagonally (!) the horse schooling area, go over two fence stiles, along the wall to an metal-bar stone stile, and finally through a wooden gate along the rear wall of the cottage (L) to a stone stile. *And that is the 'right of way'!* Then turn left to wherever you have parked your car (9.4km).

E2: Houses Hill

The Valley Round

Distance: 8km (5 miles)

Time: 2½ hours

Map: OS Landranger 110 (1:50 000), Explorer 288 (1: 25 000)

Parking: in the vicinity of St John the Baptist Church, Church Lane, Kirkheaton, grid reference: 179172

Terrain: meadow and field, woodland, farm track, path and short stretches of road – the walk is undulating with moderate ascents and descents

Refreshments: at the Beaumont Arms, Church Lane

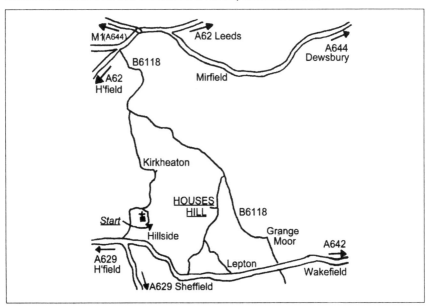

THIS walk is a very pleasant circle starting and finishing near St John the Baptist Church in Kirkheaton, passes through the hamlet of Houses Hill and village of Lepton, but skirts all other habitation. It affords very good views both ways across a valley, whilst only descending into it once. A feature of this walk is the number of old tombstones and carved pillars which have been utilised in stiles.

With the church at your back and the Beaumont Arms on your right take the track along its rear side and between walls past a stile of curved stone pillars. Go through a metal and wood pillar stile, across the field to squeeze between metal gates (L) and the parapet walls of a bridge (R) on either side of a track. Go straight on over the field alongside a stream (R); NB *the vertically laid stones on its far bank.* You come to a conically shaped upright stone squeeze stile (*an old gravestone?*). Pass through and go up between converging high walls. *On the right are ornamental gateposts of a drive leading to an imposing residence.*

Turn left onto the road, cross it and walk 70 metres until you reach the entrance to the cemetery. Turn right and make your way uphill through the cemetery and turn to the far left-hand corner, where you will find a metal gate onto a path. Turn left and go past a stone slab stile. Almost immediately, turn up on a stony slab path over a stream and through a few trees. Keep to the left-hand path with a wire fence (R) and follow the edge of the quarry to the right (1km).

Continue on still following the quarry edge round until you descend between two oak trees into a pretty little gorge. A well-built stone bridge takes you over the stream and up to wooden steps. The path bears up left between fences. At a wall end (R), turn right up alongside a hedge. When you come to a wall ahead beside a white post, turn left and follow the wall up round to the top right corner of the field, and go over a wood bar stile. *There is a fine view from here back down into the valley from which you have ascended.* Veer left following the line of the telephone cables to a wall stile, then follow the fence (L) to a wall stile. Go up a narrow path between a fence/hedge (L) and a red brick wall (R) to an iron bar red brick wall stile. Follow the hedge (L) and go past a farm and cottages (L) *with a wagon wheel on the wall of* *the last one,* to another red brick stile (2km).

At the track turn right down a hedge (L) and through a metal gate ahead. Turn left along a wall (L) to go left of a fence and along the bottom of a wood (L). Bend down right and then left through a stone slab stile and past the buildings of Hagg Farm *with an unusual bow window.* Go through metal gates onto a tarmac lane. Follow the lane straight on through the hamlet of Houses Hill turning left round Maple Farm, *which has a fine rooster weather vane on its garage.* Round left and down Long Tongue Scrog Lane – *why is it so named?* At the T-junction beside High Cross 1908 (R), turn right down the road *past Elm Facet (R) and Everlasting Springs (L).* At the bottom right bend (3km) where Healey Green Lane becomes Sands Lane, turn left up a broad track/drive through a metal gate and walk steadily uphill through the woodland until you pass a large red brick based building (L). At the top turn right onto a track which takes you alongside the wood (R).

Bow window at Hagg Farm

At a metal gate ahead veer right past a fence stile and go down for approximately 0.7km through a wood *which at first consists of coniferous trees but at the bottom changes to deciduous trees,* as you cross a stream. When you come to a hedge ahead turn right and go across a wooden bridge over another stream in front of a stone pillar and fence stile. Go up left past a post and on up the field to the right of a tree and on to a wall stile. On alongside a wall (R) and over a wall stile to the main road in Lepton. Turn left and immediately right on a

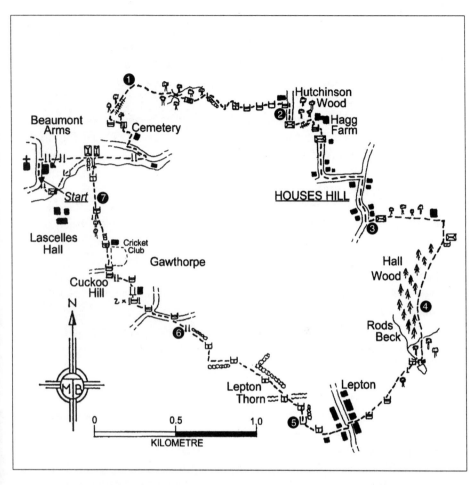

signposted path up Town Gate with a post box on the corner. Past a white cottage (L) at the top turn right between walls and over a fence stile and then diagonally left over the field to go through a gap in the wall (5km).

Turn right alongside a wall (R) to a fence stile in a hedge. Veer left to another fence stile beside a wall (R) and a third fence stile further on. When the wall turns right, the path goes straight on heading for a wall corner (R) jutting out into the field; at the corner carry on under pylon cables in the direction of Zeneca in the distance. *As you cross the field, on your left is Castle Hill just above the field line; to your right is a row of cottages, some with weavers' windows, and also the valley from where you have come.* You cross a fence stile in a wall. Go left and right round the corner of the field. At the bottom of a hedge (L) take a fence stile over the wall; follow this round left and right between stone pillars (6km).

Cross the field to where the wall (L) comes in again; follow it to a wall stile *with a thick stone pillar topped by a metal spike.* Turn left onto Lucy Lane. At the junction with Gawthorpe Lane go straight over and through a wall stile. Walk over the fields to two squeeze stone pillar and wall stiles in succession. Walk alongside a wall (R) to a stone pillar stile *with carved pillar coping stones built into the wall. On this stretch you pass a house (R) with a horse exercise ring.* Beyond the stile and halfway along the wall at a wall stile (R) veer left across to a pillar stile *(the far one is an old tombstone).* Further on there is a wall stile *made of an ornamental pillar laid flat down.* Go over the lane to a slab wall stile and along a wall (R). *Over the wall is Lascelles Hall Cricket Club.*

Beside the pavilion is a fence stile with large circular pillar and wall stile leading to stone steps down into the field (7km). Follow the line of trees (L) and as you level out, *note the imposing ornamental gateposts and side gate (L); they once led to a quarry!* Take the combined wall and fence stile beside a metal gate (R) and go down over the field towards Kirkheaton ahead. A fence stile takes you between a fence (L) and hedge (R) to a red brick parapet bridge. Squeeze left through the wall and gate. Walk along the stream *with a sluice gate (L),* through a wall gap, then a metal gate. Veer right to go through stone pillars and to wherever you parked your car (8km).

E3: Kirkburton

The Hamlets of Beldon Brook

Distance: 8km (5 miles)

Time: 2½ hours

Map: OS Landranger 110 (1:50 000), Explorer 288 (1: 25 000)

Parking: at a car park in Riley Lane in the centre of Kirkburton, grid reference: 197126

Terrain: meadow and field, woodland, farm track, path and short stretches of road – the walk is undulating with moderate ascents and descents

Refreshments: at The Royal in Riley Lane and the George Inn in George Street

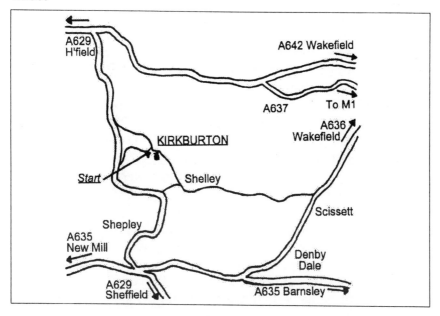

THIS pleasant and relatively easy walk starts and finishes in the centre of Kirkburton. It takes you in a wide circle around the valley of Beldon Brook, affording you fine views of the surrounding countryside as well as of the hamlets of Little Lepton and Linfit. There are also many 'points of interest' to see throughout the walk.

With the car park at your back, turn right into Riley Lane and cross it. Immediately opposite you in the wall *is an iron water hydrant plate topped with HCWW and what appears to be a 'chess horse' symbol.* Shortly further on at Beckett Cottage (L), *look left down the lane and see the hanging baskets on three 'hangers' carved with a fox and hen, horse and plough, and squirrel and nuts!* Beyond The Royal turn left into the main road. Cross the road to bear right up Hallas Road. As you bend right and start to go steeply uphill you will pass Daisy Nook Cottage (L) and, further up, an old lane, now grassed, just before The Willows (R). After passing Gregory Playing Fields (L) at the far end joining Burton Acres Lane, zigzag right and left down a line of trees and alongside a playground (L). Go through a stile made of scaffold poles and carry straight on down a path between a fence (L) and a tumbledown wall (R) to the road at the end (1km).

Turn right for 20 metres and then left over a wall stile *(with a large centre stone slab)*. Go down the field alongside a wall (L) which becomes a fence and hedge with trees. A stone pillar stile takes you left to the other side of the wall (R). At the wall ahead go right through the gap in the wall over stone slabs and follow a wall (L) down the field. You come to a stone stile made of two vertical slabs and two pillars. Veer left to go between stone pillars, one topped with a metal spike or spigot. *What was the original use of this pillar?*

As you go diagonally on down the field *look away to your right where there is a well-built stone arched bridge, and further to the right possibly a former mine adit in the angle of the brook.* Carry on to a pillar stile in front of a wooden bridge over the Beldon Brook, which meanders, in places, over a rocky bed – *the old stone clapper is now in the brook.* Veer right to a wall stile, but do NOT cross it onto a former built-up trackway. Instead, turn at right angles left and go up and across the field aiming for a mid-point in the wood ahead. You come to a fence stile, which takes you into the wood (2km).

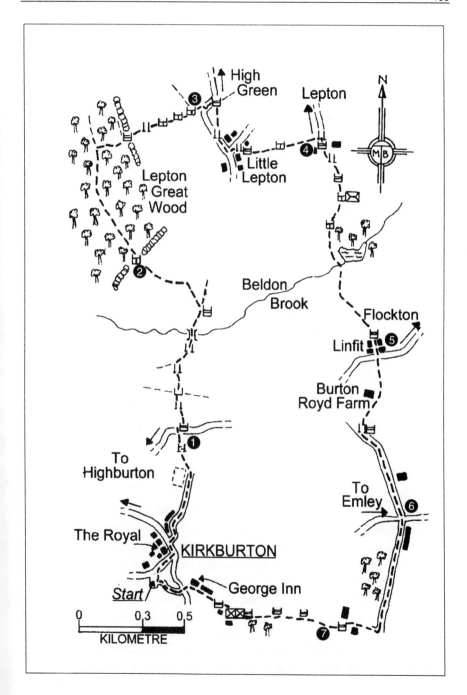

Take the route straight ahead through the wood *of deciduous trees, sycamore, oak and silver birch.* Midway through you go over a trickle of a stream and as you near the corner of the wood with daylight ahead, the paths diverge in front of you. Bear rightish and keep to the main and broadest path. Just as the path bends right and goes into a long straight stretch, turn right round a big holly bush and follow the path up, round and through the trees to a wall stile. Over this wall stile and out of the wood, go up alongside the wall (L) to a stone <u>and</u> wood pillar stile over a wall, then over stones to a fence stile. Go up the field to another fence stile, *beyond which you can see Lepton Church obliquely to your left.* Proceed straight on to a third fence stile, with a metal gate (L) (3km).

Go left up the lane for 70 metres and as it bends left, take the wall stile to the right. Carry straight on over the field along the line of power lines until you come to a pillar stile. Turn left into Green Balk Lane and go past Great Oak Barn and Cottage (L) *and the Little Folly (R) with its witch on a broom weather vane. You are now in the delightful hamlet of Little Lepton.* Turn left into Pond Lane and in 30 metres turn right in front of a stone house and go straight on between the buildings. Bear left past a red brick/stone outhouse (L) to a wall stile in the far-left corner. Proceed down the field keeping to the right-hand side wall of Low Fold Farm. Go into and out of the dip up to a fence stile beside oak trees (R). Keep alongside the fence/wall with oak trees (R) past circular pillars with metal spikes and two ornamental gateposts until you come to a stone pillar stile in the corner. Turn right down the drive of Lower House to a little stone stile at the right-hand corner of the house (4km).

Go down alongside the wall (L) and round left to ornamentally carved stone pillars on either side of a metal gate between oak trees. Squeeze between pillars, stone and metal. Turn right down alongside the hedge. At the bottom of the field there is a slab stone stile overgrown with nettles and in front of a stream/gully, so move left and up right round a hawthorn bush to follow the hedge (R) to a fence stile with iron gate (L). Carry on above the stream (R) for 80 metres: the path appears to go straight on, but go down right to the stream and a small fence stile under a willow. Over this the path goes left of a broken-down wall and a big hawthorn bush. *Down on*

The hamlet of Linfit

the left is a large pond which is part of Beldon Brook. If you are lucky (and quiet) you may espy a heron fishing here.

From hereon the path is indistinct, but bend left round the corner of the fence following its line until you see a fence stile up ahead. Once over this, head across the field for the mid-point of the wall ahead, left of a red brick outhouse, where there is a wall stile at the left side of a former, but now blocked up, gateway. Go up and over the wall stile using the wooden bar. Proceed along a wall (R) to a tarmac lane (Linfit Fold) between the buildings of Lockwood Farm. *In this hamlet of Linfit the first of the row (L) is The Mistle and the last detached is One Acre* (5km).

Down to and across the road and into the lane between walls towards Burton Royd Farm. You go past a fine stone slab stile (L) and having passed the farm (R), in the dip *note the semi-circular water trough set in the wall (R)*. At the end of the lane is a slab wall stile to the left of large and stout gateposts. Turn left up a broad track between hedges and walls. Ignore all side tracks. On the left you come to a large house, The Poplars. *At the side entrance it has some inter-*

esting features in the walls: by the left-hand gatepost an arrow, by the right-hand a rectangular hollow stone with inscribed letters and numbers on its sides; on the end wall of the garage an octagonal feature, like a font cover, and atop the garage a 'hare' weather vane. Carry on to the end of the lane with Emley Mast on your left (6km).

Over the road go up the lane passing a row of cottages (L): *on the first is the inscription 'Miles and Nancy Scafe AD 1857'; on the last house is a stone plaque with a carving of sheep.* Carry on and past a wood (R): *over the wall is a small man-made pond (only visible in the wet season).* At the top bend right with the lane and *you will see a cat (sic!) running along the roof of the house ahead, which also at its gate has a gaily painted mail box, a cartwheel and 'beware the dog' sign.* Go over a wall stile to the right of a metal gate and go along the wall (R). *You get a fine view down into another valley towards Shelley and beyond.* Go past a wall stile beside a lone stone pillar (7km).

Further on, go past a similar stile and go downhill over stone slabs through trees, *which at the right time of the year have a carpet of bluebells.* Squeeze between wooden pillars, with a farm gate (L), and through the trees go down between walls to a double wooden gate ahead. On its right, squeeze through a stone slab stile and go down a narrow path between high walls. Go through a stone pillar stile and onto a road (Lane Head Lane). At the main road by the George Inn (R) cross over and go down Low Gate past the Masonic Car Park (L) with Kirkburton Church above it. At the bottom with Treacle Cottage, Low Town (L), turn right and go straight on with the left fork down to the car park (8km).

E4: Emley

Both sides of the Ridge

Distance: 8km (5 miles)

Time: 2½ hours

Map: OS Landranger 110 (1:50 000), Explorer (1: 25 000)

Parking: in car park behind the Post Office in Church Street, grid reference: 244131

Terrain: meadow and field, farm track, path and short stretches of road — the walk is often on the flat, up and down fields, with a longish uphill stretch back into Emley. The path through Bank Wood may be very overgrown in the summer

Refreshments: food available at two public houses and restaurants: The White Horse in Beaumont Street and The Green Dragon in Church Street

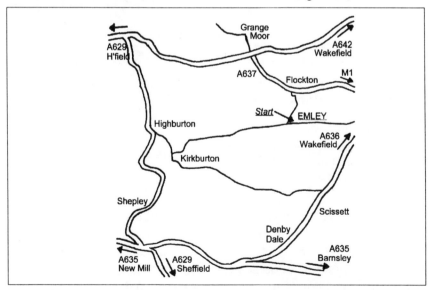

Advice: this is a walk which you may choose to do during late autumn or spring, as the stretch through Bank Wood can be overgrown with brambles and nettles during the summer. The walk is an easy stroll, starting from the well-known village of Emley which sits astride a ridge. Firstly, it gives you views north to the next ridge topped by Midgley and Flockton, takes you down into a valley, criss-crossing the Kirklees Way and through the picturesque Bank Wood before bringing you back up to the Emley ridge. You gain panoramic views over Clayton West to High Hoyland, and in particular of the Pennines in the south and west distance as you ascend back to Emley. A special feature of this walk is the stiles made of horizontal metal bars between stone posts.

Double cross in wall

From the car park exit onto Church Street turning north easterly down to the right. As the 14th century church of St Michael the Archangel comes into view (L), cross the road to look carefully at the wall surrounding its grounds. *Built into the wall you can see various relics: one is a double cross inscribed* 'RH 1683'; *another contains the words 'John Jackson, Schoolmaster, 1732, Entred, September .....'; a third inscription reads:*

    If Fortune keep thee warm
    If Friends about thee swarm
    Like bees about a Honey Pot
    but if she frown and cast thee down
    Lye there and Rott

the right-hand stone has the inscription 'Wiglesworth 1673' *above twin arches carved with the words* 'PORTA PATENS ESTO' *and* 'NULLI CLAUDARIS HONESTO': *the first might be translated as 'Let the door be open'; what does the second mean?*

    Having gazed your fill at the above, carry on down the street as it passes into Rectory Lane. This is turn becomes Clough Road, and as it bends left, beyond lamp-post no. 25, turn right through a stone stile and down stone steps to cross a stream (1km). Go up and over the top, keeping close to the hedge (R). 250 metres on you come to a stone stile with metal bars, beside a metal gate (L). Continue on following the line of the hawthorn hedge.

When you can go no further, you need to make a decision:

Shorter route: If you do this walk in the height of 'overgrown' summer, you may care to turn right at the fence stile and follow the Kirklees Way until you pick up the route later (see **Note** below).

Longer, more attractive route: If you wish to take the more attractive route, turn left along a hedge (R) and in the bottom corner go right over a metal bar stile between stone posts. Down and over the stone bridge spanning the stream, go up and straight over the field to a fence stile (2km).

At this point, don't go left on the signposted Kirklees Way, but go over the fence stile and straight on over the field. When the path meets the stream, bend round to the right with it. Soon on your left you come to a sturdy wooden bridge with handrails. Immediately having crossed it, turn right on the path that takes you into Bank Wood. The path winds round through the trees, sometimes under and over fallen ones, with the stream (R). *At various points on the opposite bank you can spot holes in its side, the habitats of various creatures.* You eventually reach a fence stile (R), which takes you down to stepping stones over the stream (3km). Bear left up the short slope and to steps down. Cross planks with a wooden handrail over the stream and to a fence stile.

[It may be that at the time of year that you do this walk the stream is high enough to be flowing over the stepping stones. In this case you may care to take an alternative route: continue walking on the original path until you reach (R) a fence stile leading on to a substantial concrete bridge with metal handrails and built on brick piers; once across the stream turn right along it until you reach the fence stile, as above].

With the fence at your back, veer diagonally right up between two trees to the tall hedges; turn right up between them and head uphill straight for the farm building at the top. Go up through the wooden gate, covered in ivy, and follow the wall (L) up and round into the driveway of Emley Woodhouse Cottage.

Note: From this point, the long and short routes combine and continue:

Kirklees Way comes in from the right. Go through the farm gate, or, if you care to, go over the unusual stone stile in the right-hand corner. At the road turn right for 20 metres, then left at the footpath sign into the farmyard; zig right and left round the barns. Take two more fence stiles in quick succession, squeeze through wooden poles and then follow the line of the hedge/fence (L) to a fence stile on the edge of the ridge (4km). *Pause to take in the panoramic views to Bretton Hall (L), to High Hoyland on the ridge ahead, and diagonally right to the windmill farm on the horizon.*

Go over the field to a fence stile in a hedge, and then veer diagonally right down to three squat trees, which may appear as one until you get close, in front of another fence stile. Cross fields to a further two fence stiles both beside metal gates (R). Carry on straight down following the line of a hedge (L) which later on becomes a wall. This brings you to a wall stile in the corner beside Gilcar Farm. Turn right up the concrete farm track between hedges until you reach the road at the end (5km).

Turn right for some 120 metres until at a lay-by (L) go through a metal gate with fence stile (L), and follow an overgrown concrete track up the field and as it bends round left in front of Emley Old Hall Farm. Now close to the hedge (L) and left of a tree and a fence stile, continue on the track past the farm (R). Go through double metal gates and on between hedges. Ignore the broad farm track (R) heading for Emley Mast, as at its top end it states 'No Right of Way'. Instead, as your track bends right, take the signposted footpath left through the metal farm gate and go past a weathered old building (R) – *note the semi-circular (dovecote?) hole above the doorway on Lady Oak Farm, and the double stone portal on its left-hand side.*

At the metal gate ahead bend right with the track. Now head straight for the Emley Moor Mast on the horizon. As the track bends left, go through a small metal gate (R) beside two farm metal gates.

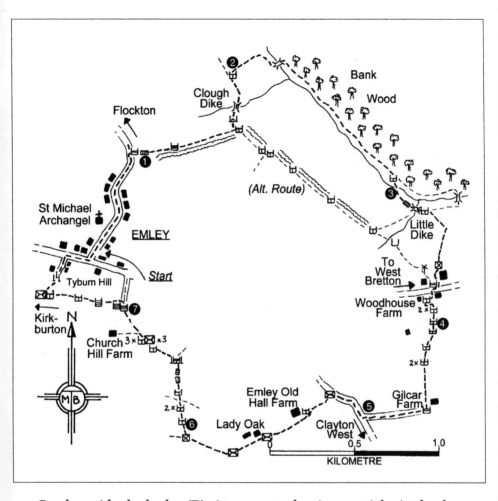

Go alongside the hedge (R). At a crosspaths signpost (6km) take the right path over the fence stile. Continue following the line of a fence/ditch/hedge (R) to two fence stiles close together in the corner. Cross a track and another fence stile, and go uphill along a hedge (R). Some 400 metres on a fence stile leads you right to planks over a stream and up stone steps to a metal bar plus fence stile between stone pillars. Veer left with the hedge (L) and go up over the crest of the rise to a fence stile *at a point where there is a conjunction of three stiles and three gates.* Continue on up the grass track which becomes a dirt track between fences past Church Hill Farm (L). Once you reach the concrete road there is a gate with fence and ladder stiles on the left (7km).

Immediately take the fence or ladder stile (L) in front of the houses; just beyond them ignore the stile (R), continuing on the level along the hedge (R) and over a fence stile. *As you walk along this stretch, do take the opportunity to take in the vista: from the Emley Mast straight ahead and slightly left to Black Hill and Holme Moss in the far south westerly distance and to the Pennines leading over into the Derwent Valley way beyond the windmill farm.* You come to another wooden ladder stile and further on a fence stile. After another fence stile beside a metal gate (L), you need to turn up right onto a track between hedges and go on through three metal posts. Take the tarmac road past no. 36 with high on its front wall the inscription:

S
J M
1839

Carry on up Tyburn Lane past houses (R) variously named Manderley, Four Winds and Grey Gables until you come out on the main road (Beaumont Street) opposite The White Horse. Turn right and at the crossroads ahead *you see the remains of the old market cross, painted white.* Just as you turn left into Church Street, *glance to your right to view the former Reading Room, dated 1879, now named 'Wysholme'.* Now return to wherever you have parked your car (8km).

E5: Shepley

The Walk of the Weather Vanes

Distance: 7.2km (4½ miles)

Time: 2 hours

Map: OS Landranger 110 (1:50 000), Explorer (1: 25 000)

Parking: in the vicinity of The Black Bull in Marsh Lane

Starting Point: in Marsh Lane at the junction with A629, grid reference: 193097

Terrain: fields, farm tracks, lanes and some stretches of road – the walk is undulating and moderately easy with ascents at the beginning and in the middle

Refreshments: The Black Bull in Shepley, The Sovereign at A629/635 crossroads, The Star in Upper Cumberworth

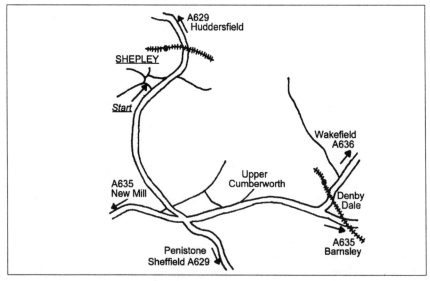

THIS walk starts and ends in the village of Shepley. It takes you high up giving you on a clear day some superb views to the furthest parts of West Yorkshire. It also takes you down into pleasant valleys of the Dearne tributaries, and through the attractive village of Upper Cumberworth. Look out for the weather vanes which depict the life of this part of the country, and also for many interesting features including quaint cottage names. You will also see some fine examples of architecture in buildings of varying ages from the early 1600s onwards.

Facing east cross the main road (A629) and go up the lane opposite between walls and past the school playground and fields (R). Go straight on up through the trees; halfway up and slightly to the right you come, rather surprisingly, to a war memorial together with seats. Rejoin the path and continue straight ahead over a wall stile and across the field to a further wall stile close to the right-hand corner. Then keep the wall on your right until you come to a metal kissing gate in the top corner. Go left and down over the stone slabs to turn right and pass in front of the cottages. This private drive, which is a right of way, takes you past a large stone house and pond (L). Halfway up by a metal gate (L) is a wall stile. Go over it and head diagonally across the field to a wall stile left of a tree (1km).

Turn left into Carr Lane. *Carr may be 'a boggy or fenny copse, grown up with low bushes, willows, alders, etc'., or what else can 'Carr' mean?* After 80 metres cross the road and take a wall stile (R). The path heads off diagonally to the left following the line of a collapsed wall to a wall/fence stile overhung by trees. Continue uphill, aiming for the left-hand end of a stand of fir trees to a wall stile. Cross the stile and walk up the field towards the buildings ahead, alongside a partly collapsed wall and gateposts with slot holes (R). At the tarmac drive, turn right up it. At the road turn right for 10 metres, cross and take the path uphill to the right of the cottages (10A The Barn). This leads initially between a wall (L) and a fence (R) and then, after some steps, between walls, the path being overhung by trees.

At the top, step over a low wall stile into the road and turn left for 20 metres. Cross the road and enter a field by a wall stile to the left of

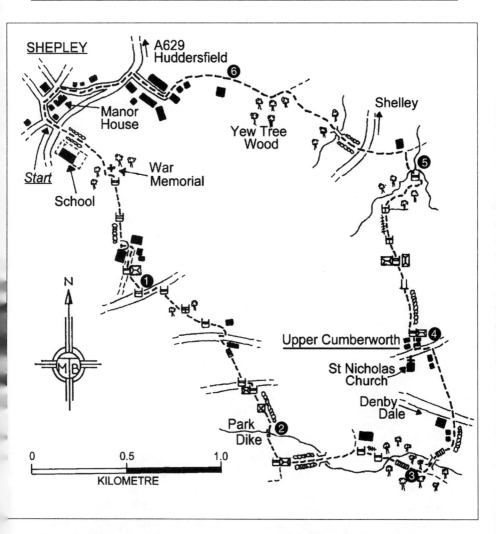

a metal farm gate. Keep straight ahead, with the wall (L). At the next field boundary, pass through a small gate to the left of a metal farm gate and continue down the field, still keeping the wall (L) – *halfway down an unusual stone pillar is set in the wall.* At the line of haw-thorn trees, the path bends right and drops to cross Park Dike via stepping stones (2km). Go straight on keeping the wall (R), and walk across the field to a wall still with a gate (L). Turn left into Park Lane. After a zigzag left and right, the lane flattens out and crosses a stream. At this point look over the walls: *(L) you will see a well-built stone arched tunnel over the stream, (R) there is a small waterfall over rock slabs.*

At the left bend in the lane, take the footpath (R) over a wall stile onto the Dearne Way, signmarked by a miner's lamp. With a fence on your left go over another wall stile into Upper Dearne Woodlands. Keeping to the right-hand track, take the stepping stones over the stream and ascend the bankside on stone steps (3km). The track goes down through the beech trees until you come to a wooden bridge over the stream which takes you up via stone steps on to a lane left up between walls. Go up round to the left and past Thimble Cottage until you come to the main road (A635).

Cross straight over and bear left up the footpath – possibly after resting a while on the seat (R). The path takes you past a fancy treehouse in a garden (L) and up between walls, *topped with half pipes,* and holly hedges. You will reach Eunice Lane at the point where Salt Pie Cottage stands as the first cottage of a row. At the road junction turn left into Upper Cumberworth and walk 50 metres to St

Stocks at St Nicholas' Church

Nicholas' Church (4km) *with its extensive graveyard (L) and fine rooster weather vane – also take the time to walk round to the main door where stand the ancient stocks.* [The Star is 250 metres further on across the main road]. Opposite the church, cross the road turning right into Balk Lane. You now pass a cluster of renovated cottages, *one with steps leading up to a loft.* Go straight ahead between the buildings until you come to an unusual wall stile beside a metal gate (R).

Take the time to pause here and enjoy your fill of the vast panoramic view. To the west you will see the bluff below Thurstonland, and panning round eastwards the church spire at Thurstonland, Castle Hill and (on a clear day) further northwards to Halifax and beyond, Emley Mast and beyond to Wakefield, to High Hoyland and Barnsley in the east. Once sated with the view step left over the stile in between the walls and down the field keeping the wall on your right to firstly a stone pillar stile and then a wall stile in the angle of two metal gates. Next over a fence/wall stile, keeping the fence now to the left, and then over a fence stile into a copse. Wind round and down between the trees and streams to a wall stile which takes you out of the copse and over a stream (5km).

Take the lane left and turn left up past the cottages (R). Carry on until you come to the road. Cross onto a public bridleway and going between walls you cross a stream *on a strongly built and dressed stone bridge.* The path takes you up between a mixture of holly hedges, walls, two opposing metal gates and fences. Follow the path right and then left round the angle of a wood (L). Bend right and along a flat section (6km) *which shows signs of having once had a narrow-gauge railtrack for mining wagons.*

Emerging past Briar Lodge (L), take the road (The Knowle) straight on. *Just before the left bend look to see another weather vane, of a horse and ploughman, and before the right bend in the last garden on the left is another treehouse.* Bend right with the road between the factories and offices. At the road junction, *the house on the right has blocked up windows on its rear, whilst the house on the left (The Abbey) is a fine example of the Georgian era.* Go left at the main road (A629) for 100 metres and cross right to pass a triangular milestone *showing Huddersfield 7 miles to the north and Penistone 5½ miles to the south.*

Bear right down Lydgate Road: *in the bottom is a renovated house (R) with weavers windows in its second storey. You may be wondering why the walk brings you back into the thick of habitation. Well, just carry on to the top of the road* (7km), *turn left and halfway along is the surprise of the walk! Opposite an imposing Victorian house (R) is an original Manor House (L), somewhat hidden behind a rather dilapidated stone wall. It dates almost back to Elizabethan times as shown on the lintel over the magnificent entrance door, inscribed 'ANNO DOMINI 1608'. Just beyond is the Granary.* Follow the road round to the left and The Black Bull, and wherever you have parked your car (7.2km).

E6: Quaker Settlement

The Friends Meeting

Distance: 6km (3¾ miles)

Time: 2 hours

Map: OS Landranger 110 (1:50 000), Explorer 288 (1: 25 000)

Parking: in a lay-by facing west on A635 just west of the railway viaduct at Denby Dale, grid reference: 225083

Terrain: path, farm track, short stretches of road, field and woodland — the walk is undulating with a steepish ascent up to and descent from the area of High Flatts

Refreshments: not available on the walk but possible in Denby Dale and Upper Cumberworth

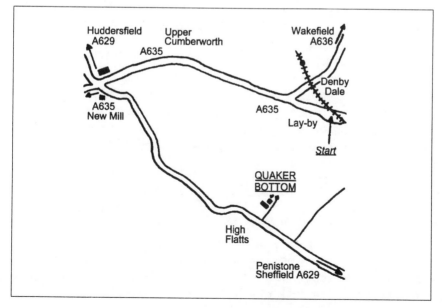

THIS walk provides you with a number of charming features. It takes you through pleasant countryside up and around the interesting Quaker Settlement and brings you back down through a delightful stretch of the Upper Dearne Woodland.

Take the A635 in a westward direction until you come to a lane which veers up left and displays a 'Polite – No Parking' notice. Continue uphill and bend left with the lane at Toby Wood Farm (1km) past a long low barn *dated 1554*.

At the T-junction carry straight on between walls and over a wall stile to the right of a wooden farm gate. Bend left and past two ponds (L) and a small reservoir (R), following the wall round to the right. Go over a sturdy stone stile and up the field to a wall stile at the left-hand edge of a wood – *note that the bottom slab is a old gatepost*. Go along the edge of the wood on the right-hand side of a wall. Exit from the wood over a tumbledown wall and go up over the field towards stone houses. Continue uphill left past a tree and bend left up to a fence stile (2km).

Down on the right nestles a small reservoir in a fold of land. You can also see St Nicholas' Church at Upper Cumberworth peeping over the horizon (R). Proceed to the wall stile (R) and follow the wall to the lane. Cross the lane and zigzag right and left. Go over a wall stile and over paving stones to a fence gate between stone pillars. Stone steps take you down to cross the stream and over slabs to five steps upwards and through a metal gate and on up a grassy path. *Over the wall (R) there is a gem of a rock garden.* Go up between stone walls and under a wooden bridge to a flight of stone steps and a kissing gate. *Over the wall (L) are two stone water troughs.*

You emerge into the Settlement at Quaker Bottom: *the Friends Meeting House, Low House Farm Cottage with the inscription EDS 1717 over the doorway, Low House Farm with a cock weather vane, the Carriage House and Green Hollows.* Go left up the lane and at the top turn right onto the main road (A629) and past the quaintly named Pump Row Cottages – *how did they come by this name?* On the left bend, take the footpath to the right; it bends right and past a seat, to follow the wall into the left corner (3km).

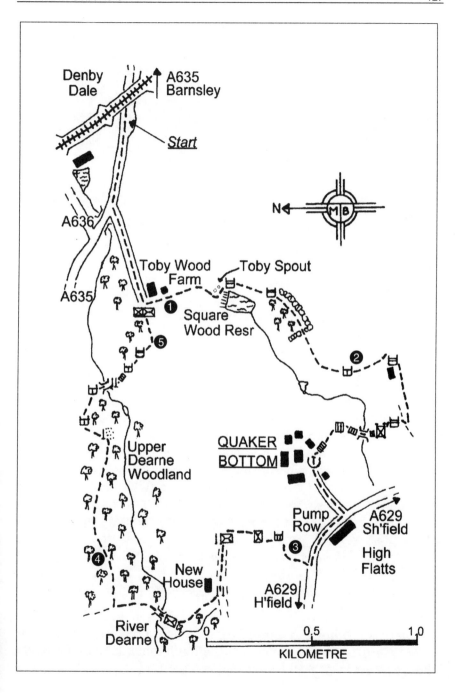

Upper Dearne woodland

Go left over a metal rail at a slab stile and down the field with a wall (R). Halfway downhill turn right through a metal gate and proceed down between a hedge (L) and a wall (R). Bend left to go between stone pillars beside a metal gate (R). Go left into the lane. *On the end of the barn, note the twin dovecote (now blocked up).* As the lane bends left, go off right beside a stream, through a squeeze stile and along a path beside trees. Bend round to the right and just past the confluence of two streams, squeeze past a metal gate and take a stepping stone bridge left over the stream. Take the path up right and alongside a wall (R). *Here is a superb example of gateposts with pole slots, and also there is an animal hole through the wall at the bottom of a post.* At the end of the wall turn sharp right into Upper Dearne Woodland. The slightly lower path takes you through the middle of the wood (4km).

There is a number of bird boxes high up on the trees and, at the right time of the year, a profusion of daffodils and rhododendrons. (At the crosspaths you can carry straight on and take the stepping stones over the stream and see *to the right a stone overflow ladder to the stream below*. There is no easy way beyond this point.) Back at a wooden post with a pile of stones beyond it, veer left to a fence stile *with its original metal posts*. Turn right down the lane and in 100 metres take the fence stile across a wooden bridge and past leaning stone pillars. Go up the stone steps to a fence stile in the wall. Veer diagonally left up the field to a wall stile, into the wood and over a stream. Carry on up the path until it joins a path from the right. Walking left you come to a fence gate beside a wooden farm gate (R) (5km).

Walk on back down the lane. At the junction with the main road, on the left *look at the tunnel of dressed stone with keystones which takes the stream under the road. On the far side of the road there is an interesting set of channels feeding water to the mill further down.* As you return to wherever you have parked your car, you gain a fine view of the railway viaduct – *the present Victorian structure replaced an earlier wooden viaduct which was in danger of collapse* (6km).

E7: Denby Dale

The Denby Trio Walk

Distance: 9km (5½ miles)

Time: 3 hours

Map: OS Landranger 110 (1:50 000), Explorer 288 (1: 25 000)

Parking and Starting Point: in the vicinity of Exley Gate on Dry Hill Lane, 500 metres in the direction of Clayton West and High Hoyland, from the 'Dunkirk Inn' junction (A635), Lower Denby, grid reference: 242083

Terrain: meadow and field, farm track, path and some stretches of road/lane – the walk is undulating with moderate up and downhill stretches

Refreshments: the Dunkirk Inn (A635), Lower Denby

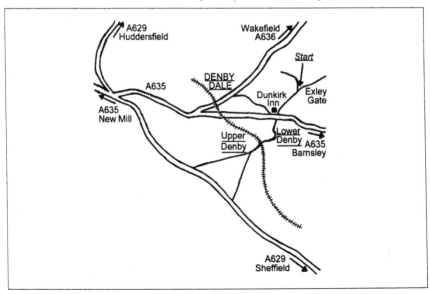

THIS walk takes you through a variety of pleasant countryside around the 'Denbys', i.e. Denby Dale, Upper and Lower Denby, including Denby Hall. On the return you go up the ancient stone paved trackway to Gunthwaite and a fine example of a black and white timbered and stone barn.

Starting at Exley Gate go in a north easterly direction towards High Hoyland and pass a Service Reservoir (L). Almost immediately, opposite a camping ground go right over a wall stile onto a public footpath, keeping a wall (R). *You get a wide view over to Barnsley on your left.* Continue on to a wall stile, then veer left across a field heading for Denby Hall farm in the distance to an wide metal gateway at the corner of two hedges. Keeping to the hedge (L) go on past the farm tips through an open gate to a lane by Denby Hall (*rebuilt 1923*) (1km).

Turn right for 35 metres, then turn left onto a footpath and on through a metal gate and past buildings to a gate, with a wall stile (L) against the building and a pond (R). Follow the path along the hedge (L) to a fence stile and then a wall stile. Keeping the fence on your left, after a boggy stretch you go over a stream (dry in summer), through a small gate or over a wall stile into Deffer Wood. Wind your way bending round right and then left – this stretch could be muddy after rain. At a six-way crosstracks (2km), take the second track on the right and on to a T-junction at the far side of the wood. *Here you get a fine view over Cawthorne to Barnsley and to a summer house at the top corner of the field (L) beside the wood.*

Turn right down a path. Further on cross a stream and go to the corner of the wood at Susannah Spring – *why so called?* Before a gate go left over a wall, and straight over the field to the corner of the wood. Do not go over the fence stile, but turn right following the hedge (L) to bend left over a fence stile, beside a metal gate (R). Continue along the hedge and at a wooden farm gate ahead veer right, following the hedge round left to a fence stile by holly (L) and hawthorn (R) (3km). Go down along the hedge (L) and over a fence stile to the road (A635).

Cross the road and go over a wall stile onto a footpath (Kirklees Way), keeping left of a henhouse. Take the metal footbridge over a stream and veer right up a steep track to a wall and then a fence stile by a holly bush. Follow a hedge and wall (L) up to a stepped wall stile in front of a cottage in the top corner. Go through the garden to a wall stile and over a third wall stile onto a track. Turn left down the track, then round right and left. Take the left fork uphill and follow the wall (L) for approximately 0.7km up to the top of the wood.

Where the track goes left turn right over a wall stile onto a footpath, going straight across and down over a field to join a wall (R) and a wall stile; skirt the hollow on your right. Follow a wall (R) until on your right you cross a wall stile with wood beams on its far side. Veer down past gorse and hawthorn bushes (R) to cross a stone slab bridge over a stream (5km). Go over a large stone slab and along a wall in front of farm buildings to a wall stile. Turn left, round the back of an outbuilding, and left to take the high wall stile into the lane. Turn right past an old beamed shed (R). *Just up on your left is a gate which has a corn quern as the base of its steps: take care, if you go through this gate, as just inside (L) down behind a crumbling wall is an old iron overshot water wheel. As you go up the lane you can see the former mill race (L) now dried up.* Go on through a gate and wall stile, and up onto the road.

Opposite a pond (L) see (if not overgrown in summer) how the wall (R) is built on top of the natural rock of a small quarry. At the junction of three roads take the public footpath straight ahead veering right up Gunthwaite Lane: *this is an ancient paved trackway with the stones scored to help the animals from slipping.* The lane goes up for a considerable distance between walls. At Gunthwaite Hall, *the left corner building has mullion and dovecote windows on its end wall. Take the time to go up Gunthwaite Lane to look left back at the stone and black and white timbered barn.* Then retrace your steps to turn left along Coach Gate lane for approximately 0.8km.

(7km) Turn left onto a farm track past a post box (R), down and through the trees over a stream. Go up and round the left bend and, before the farm, veer left through a wide gap. Follow the wall (R) past the farm and barns along a hedge (R). Go to and cross a wall stile into the wood. Veer right downhill to a fence stile. Go left over wooden planks across a stream and up along the tree hedge (L) to a wall stile at the top of the field (8km).

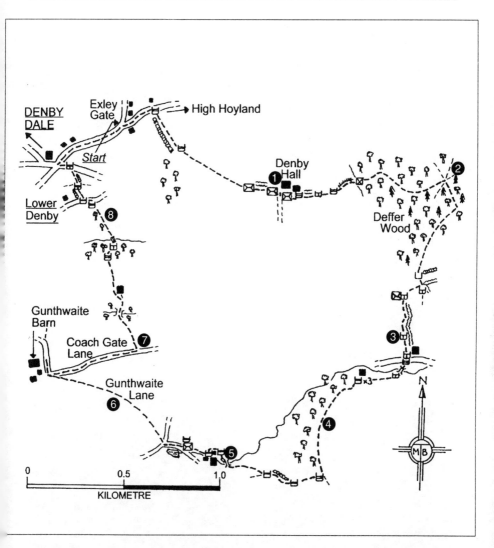

Turn left for 35 metres – *Lower Denby, 1988 Britain in Bloom village, is just up ahead.* Turning right over a wall stile, go up the field along a wall (L) to a wall/fence stile. Continue across the field along the wall (R) to a fence/wall stile. Turn left on A635 for 50 metres to the Dunkirk Inn, *with the inscription HTM 1840 – why called 'Dunkirk'?* Cross the road and turn right into Dry Hill Lane and up to Exley Gate and wherever you have parked your car (9km).

Denby Dale

The village has the famous landmark of a viaduct carrying the railway from Penistone to Huddersfield; it is now of stone (opened 1880), but originally was of timber (1850).

Denby Dale possibly owes its existence to the large ovens where earthenware pipes were manufactured. It has a village hall known as the Pie Hall; in front of it is a flowerbed planted in the world's largest pie dish, 18 feet long. Denby Dale also derives its fame from its pies, but only nine have been made in over two hundred years:

The first pie celebrated the return to sanity of George III in 1788

The second pie commemorated the defeat of Napoleon at Waterloo in 1815

The fourth pie, made for Queen Victoria's Golden Jubilee in 1887, went bad as it was baked in new wood and had to be destroyed

... and the ninth pie, the Bicentenary Pie of 1988, contained 3000kg of beef and potatoes.

The stone, black and white timbered Gunthwaite Barn – plus cat

E8: Bagden

The Mine

Distance: 7.3km (4½ miles)

Time: 2 hours

Map: OS Landranger 110 (1:50 000), Explorer 288 (1: 25 000)

Parking: travelling on A635 from Denby Dale, just past the Dunkirk Inn turn left into Dry Hill Lane for 350 metres towards Exley Gate, where take the left fork following the lane round to the left for some 400 metres to park in a lay-by on the left at grid reference: 2380867

Terrain: meadow and field, woodland, farm track, path and short stretches of road – the walk is undulating with a couple of short steepish ascents

Refreshments: not available on the walk, but at the Travellers Rest (A636) and the Dunkirk Inn (A635)

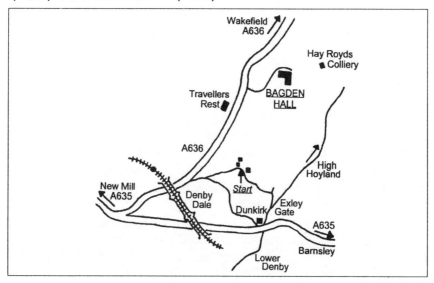

THIS is a walk which provides a variety of scenery. It takes you along several paths not often frequented. It starts by taking you alongside a tributary of the River Dearne close to Bagden Hall, now a country club with golf course and restaurant, before taking you up past a small working mine and down through Deffer Wood. It returns via Denby Hall and the ridge which runs from Lower Denby to High Hoyland.

Having parked your car in the lay-by cross the road and go down a lane opposite which bends sharp past Pingle Nook Forge (L). *A 'pingle' can mean 'a keen contest or struggle', 'a small enclosed piece of land, a paddock' or 'a small pan or cooking-pot of tinned iron, having a long handle': which is the appropriate meaning for Nook Forge?* At the brow of the lane, take a path dropping down to the left along the wood-edge (L). Follow it as it winds down between lines of trees. At the bottom, turn right to go alongside the stream (tributary of the Dearne). *There is a rocky escarpment (R) and up (L) on the main road (A636) is the Travellers Rest, accessible by a path (L) further on.*

Ignore three bridges from the left and pass cottages including Baybrook (R). Turn right at the last cottages and cross a wall stile to left of three coal bunkers. A few yards ahead across the field, turn right to join a steep track ascending from the left. At the cattle grid and wooden gate bear left round the house *with its horse and rider weather vane* to a white pillar stile (R). Go through this across the field, keeping left of the pond and tree to join a track which goes left through a white kissing gate to the right of a wooden farm gate (1km).

As you walk along you get a good view of Emley Mast (L). The broad track takes you slightly right and on to yet another white kissing gate with a fence gate between ornamental pillars (L). Bear left between cottages and follow the lane on between a metal fence (L) and a hedge of mixed hawthorn and holly (R). As you pass a farm and lodge (L) you come to the edge of Bagden Hall golf course. *Note the carved heads mounted on top of the garden wall of Bagden Lodge (L).* Turn right up the lane, following it left and up round right and left again. The track levels out and dips before going left between parapet-type walls with solid coping stones. *This structure spans the drainage outflow, culverted on the uphill side, for a small working*

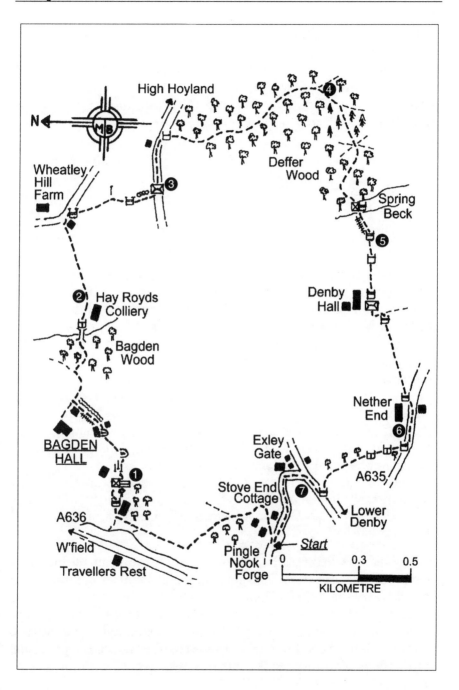

mine, visible through the trees (R). Go over a fence stile and carry on up the track past the mine, Hay Royds Colliery (2km). The mine has the distinction of being the most westerly pit still working in West (or South) Yorkshire.

As you come to the crest of the hill you can see away left *the black and white timbered gable end of Wheatley Hill Farm (1651)*. At the track end turn right past the lodge into the road for 40 metres. Then take a wall pillar stile (R). A way-marking post is visible on the sky-line beyond a wooden pylon. When this is reached, *look back at the panoramic view to the north*. Then a further post comes into view pointing the path to a pillar wall stile in the right-hand corner of the field. The path now goes uphill, following the wall (L). Go through a metal gate onto the road and turn left to Deffer Wood (3km).

Turn right into the wood over a wall stile with metal bars. *Deffer Wood is a mixed woodland of oak, beech, silver birch, sycamore and holly, with rhododendrons and bluebells colouring it at times*. Continue on down the main path for approximately 0.8km, ignoring all side tracks until you come to a waymarked Y-junction: take the right-hand fork down into the dip and as you come out, again take the right fork (4km) round and up an incline under closely over-hanging trees, mainly evergreens. At a six-way crossing, keep straight ahead following an arrow, initially along the edge of the wood (R) – a boggy stretch – then round left until you emerge from the wood over a wall stile beside a fence gate (R). Cross the small stream immediately outside the wood (dry in summer) and continue up the field alongside a fence (R). *Take in the view across to Barnsley to the far left, Hoylandswaine to the south and the windmills above Ingbirchworth ahead*. Go over a wall stile beside a metal gate (R) (5km).

Follow the hedge (R) and go alongside the farm buildings of Denby Hall. There is a stone stile in the right-hand corner up against the farm building. Before the storage tanks *you get a glimpse of the Hall (R)*. At the lane turn left between walls for 80 metres, and go over a wall stile (R). Technically the path goes straight over the field to the far left corner, but you may care to go left round the perimeter of the field, avoiding the line of a water-course by keeping a small

Working mine – Hay Royds Colliery

stand of willows on your left. A wall stile takes you onto the road opposite Nether End Farm (6km).

Take the road right past Manor House Farm (R) until you come to a public footpath sign in front of trees. A wall stile (R) takes you quickly to a fence stile (L). Follow the line of the gully and hedge (L) to cross a fence stile in the hedge. The way is technically straight ahead via a double and then a single pylon, but again you may care to veer right and up along the line of trees. A wall stile takes you onto the road (Dry Hill Lane): turn right and past a seat (L) veering up the left fork at Exley Gate. *Emley Mast appears over the horizon beyond Skelmanthorpe.* After High Field Farm (R) the main road bends left (7km).

As you go down the road, *you may be able to see the broom bushes and the silver birches in the little valley garden (R) of Stove End Cottage* before you reach your car (7.5km).

E9: Cawthorne

The Cannon Hall Round

Distance: 8km (5 miles)

Time: 2½ hours

Map: OS Sheet 110 (1:50 000), Explorer 288 (1: 25 000)

Parking: as appropriate in the village of Cawthorne or at Cannon Hall car park (pay)

Starting Point: All Saints Church, Cawthorne, grid reference 285080; or, in car park, Cannon Hall, grid reference: 273080

Terrain: meadow, field, farm track, paths and short stretches of road – the walk is moderate with one longish ascent and descent

Refreshments: food available all day at the Spencer Arms, Cawthorne, or during daytime hours at the Cannon Hall Garden Centre

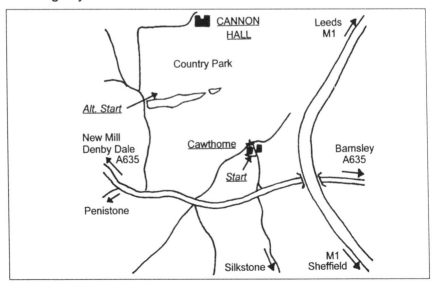

THIS walk is centred on one of the most picturesque villages in Yorkshire and takes you up on to a high ridge with extensive views in all directions. It gives you fleeting glimpses of Cannon Hall from all angles before returning you through the Country Park to your start. If you have time, the Cawthorne Museum in Lane Head Road and Cannon Hall are worth a visit.

From the top of Church Street enter the church grounds. At the west side of the tower turn left. *Immediately on your right pause to have a look at a stone mausoleum which is dedicated to the Spencer Stanhope family of Cannon, Horsforth and Banks Halls – the coat of arms can be seen on the west side. On the left-hand side of the path by the steps you can see an old Anglican cross with carvings at its bottom end.* Then continue down the path between the trees. Turn left into the road at the bottom and in 80 metres turn right into a public bridleway. Go over the stream down the lane between the railings, fence and trees; follow it round through the buildings to the signpost at the end. Go past the sign into the field and turn right to a fence gate *– the path takes you to a fine example of a clapper bridge over Tanyard Beck.* After the clapper bridge, take an acute turn left alongside a stream (L). Before a wide stone bridge (1km) veer right over a fence stile keeping the stream on your left. After a wooden bridge over a stream, turn left and go over a metal bridge. The way is straight ahead with the trees (L) across the field to a fence stile beside a metal gate.

Proceed straight on upwards. After crossing two more fence stiles (2km) you enter a wood of birch and fir. Another fence stile takes you out of the wood; you need to bear left across the field slightly to the right of a tall tree on the horizon and directly for the highest point of the ridge as it comes into view. After the fence stile, bear diagonally down the field to a wall stile beside a gate into the wood. You should wind your way upwards, straight on ignoring the tracks to the right and left, across a wide woodland track, and diagonally left up a rather muddy section between fir trees to a fence stile at the top right (3km).

The way is straight across and up the field towards a gate in front of the white bungalow. Up steps to cross the stone stile and turn left on to the road. *(50 metres to the right is the 1890 Primitive Methodist Chapel, now converted into a house). If you look back down the field you have just crossed, you will see a sign on a post that you should have bewared the 'bull in the field' – let's hope you did! Don't miss the opportunity in the next 120 metres to take in the magnificent view from east of Barnsley across to Hoyland Swaine in the west.* Immediately past Greenland Cottages take the footpath right up the track between walls overgrown with bushes: ignore the path from the right and take the next fence stile on the left to cross the field to a stone stile on the edge of a copse. Cross this avoiding the watery patches and holly bushes, over a fence stile into a field and to a ditch with another fence stile beyond. Then go diagonally up the field to the fence road stile.

Turning left onto Hollin House Lane you are now on the Kirklees Way (4km) *and soon to your right you will enjoy fine views of the valley over to Emley Moor Mast.* You have to walk some way along this road, straight on at the cross-roads onto Bagden Lane, past Toppitt Farm and Cottage and up to the top where a footpath signposts you left into Deffer Wood. *This is a wood full of fir and beech trees with a ground covering of rhododendrons. 250 metres down the track there is a seat (L) for you to rest your feet a while.* When ready to carry on, ignore the tracks from the left until you come to a signpost; take the left hand fork (5km) following it round to a stone stile.

Once in the field, *do glance up left to the top and see a delightful summer house which has a wonderful view down over the estate of Cannon Hall.* The path goes down with the stream on the right, (but not through the gate), until you cross it via a stone stile and reach a fence stile by the farm buildings of Jowett House *with its interesting mixture of building styles.. Go down the lane between the walls until you reach the crossroads (6km).*

Turn left along the road to join Bark House Lane *(pausing to view the water tank (L) made of bricks with stone surround)* down to Cannon Hall car park. If continuing on, you can make your way back to Cawthorne on either side of the lake *and you gain a fine view of Cannon Hall (L).* If on the north side, turn left at the bottom of the car park before the road bridge and go along the lake side. *Glance back to*

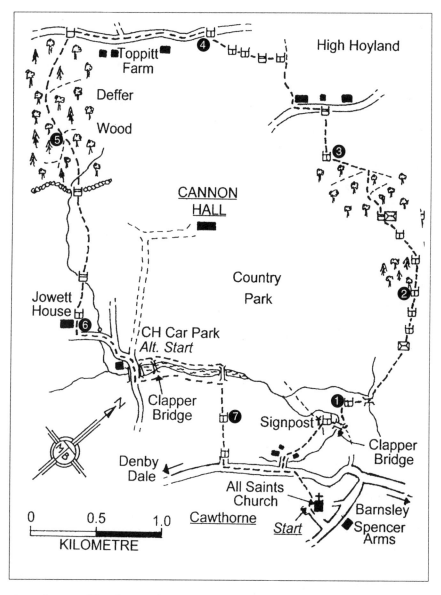

view the road bridge – what is that style of bridge called? You can either cross the lake in some 150 metres by a clapper bridge or go to the far end of the first lake before turning right over a bridge. Alternatively, you can take the narrow road bridge to the south side and turn left through a kissing gate and follow the lake (L). At its far end with a bridge (L), turn right and go slightly uphill to a fence gate (7km).

Take the paved track over the top of the field to another fence gate and into the road (The Park). At the end turn left into the main road *by a little old cottage (L)* and walk until you reach the track on the right which leads up to the Church tower and to wherever you parked your car (8km).

Cawthorne Museum

Created from two small cottages, timbered inside, it contains village relics of the distant and recent past, ranging from coal fossils to one of Hitler's bombs (!)

It is open from Easter to October on Saturday, Sunday afternoons and Bank Holidays from 2 to 5 pm. Parties catered for (01226 790545).

Cannon Hall

Dating from late 17th century this Georgian mansion was remodelled by John Carr of York in mid 18th century. Since 1957 it has been open as a country house museum containing many exhibits of furnishings, Flemish paintings, pottery/pewter and Barnsley glassware, and memorabilia of 13-18 Royal Hussars (Queen Mary's Own). The 70 acres of the country parkland were landscaped by Richard Woods in the 1760s and now afford good strolling around the ornate gardens and the 'cascade ponds'.

Also of Interest:

WEST YORKS WALKS: CALDERDALE & BRADFORD

Martin Brewis

26 circular walks which explore the dramatic landscape of Calderdale and Bradford. Surprisingly this includes rolling Pennine moorland, secluded dales, deans and cloughs and farming villages around Todmorden, Sowerby and Hebden Bridge, Haworth and Ilkley.

Detailed routes are complemented by 'points of interest' for the inquisitive walker. £6.95

BEST TEA SHOP WALKS IN WEST YORKSHIRE

Norman & June Buckley

A further volume in the now well-established tea shop walks series, covering part of the South Pennine area of first-class walking country, linked with selected tea shops in the towns and villages.

Easy-going walks are complemented by enjoyable and unusual tea shops en route. Full descriptions are given of the tempting delicacies that await the hungry walker. £6.95

TOWNS AND VILLAGES OF BRITAIN: WEST YORKSHIRE

John Spencer

This title is the essential guide to West Yorkshire as seen through the colourful history of its towns and villages. Although written in a lively, readable style, it's comprehensive and presented in an easy-to-use reference book format. Over 300 entries cover all the main settlements of the county, highlighting the key buildings, landscape and famous personalities of the area, together with associated folklore and legends.

£7.95

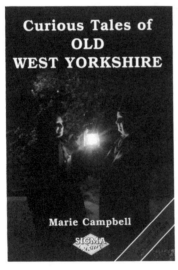

CURIOUS TALES OF OLD WEST YORKSHIRE

Marie Campbell

"A fascinating collection of odd tales of occult doings, curious clergymen, eccentrics and the allsorts of society's fringes." NORTHERN EARTH 1999

"In this fascinating, entertaining, bustling...package of oddities, Marie Campbell ranges far and wide." BRADFORD TELEGRAPH & ARGUS

£7.95

All of our books are available through booksellers. In case of difficulty, or for a free catalogue, please contact:

SIGMA LEISURE, 1 SOUTH OAK LANE, WILMSLOW, CHESHIRE SK9 6AR.
Phone: 01625-531035
Fax: 01625-536800.
E-mail: info@sigmapress.co.uk
Web site: http//www.sigmapress.co.uk
MASTERCARD and VISA orders welcome.